Presented to:

_____

Presented by:

_____

Date:

_____

E-MAIL FROM GOD FOR TEENS

by

Claire Cloninger & Curt Cloninger

Honor Books
Tulsa, Oklahoma

E-Mail from God for Teens, clothbound
ISBN 1-56292-930-5
Copyright © 1999 by Claire Cloninger & Curt Cloninger

Published by Honor Books
P.O. Box 55388
Tulsa, Oklahoma 74155

DEDICATION

For Kaylee and Caroline

Also for Jeanne, Claire, Anna, Jesse, Kitty, David, Edward,
Patrick, Pamela, Erin Claire, Daniel D., Chuck, Bonnie, and Leah

INTRODUCTION

Do you picture God as an old man with a white beard, drifting through the sky and dropping gloom and doom on the world? Do you see Him as a preacher in a three-piece suit, pounding a pulpit and yelling at the people in the pews? If so, I have good news for you! God isn't anything like those old stereotypes. He's real. He's alive. He knows your name. And He loves you!

Suppose you could sit in a chat room with God every day and ask Him anything. Suppose you could hear Him talking to you about your problems, your friendships, and all the decisions you have to make. You can! You can hear Him through His Word.

E-Mail From God for Teens speaks God's words in everyday language. It offers guidance, help, hope, good news, encouragement, and love. It's a chance for you to log on to God's heart and mind. So, what are you waiting for?

YOU WON'T MISS OUT

LORD, you have assigned me my portion and my cup;
you have made my lot secure.
The boundary lines have fallen for me in pleasant places;
surely I have a delightful inheritance.

Psalm   16:5-6

Dear Child,

>Lots of people think that being a Christian means missing out on the good stuff. They think I'm the father who makes you ride your bike to school on your sixteenth birthday when everyone else gets a new car.

That's not Me. I have a wonderful inheritance for you. Read My will and learn that I've promised you the best slice of life. I've made you, so I know what makes you happy. I know you better than you know yourself.

So hang in there and trust Me. I've got something great for you, and it's not a rusty bicycle, I assure you. I'm the One Who knows how to bless you.

Your Maker,
>God

== == ==   == == == == == == == == ==

YOU ARE GIFTED FOR A REASON

Be generous with the different things God gave you, passing them around so all get in on it.

1 Peter 4:10 | THE MESSAGE

Dear Child,

>Ever think of the billions of people I've already made and wonder why I needed you? Is there a real purpose for your life? Trust Me, I gave every person special gifts—you included. Maybe you haven't found yours yet, but you will.

Some people are good managers. Some are good artists, or athletes, or teachers, or writers. I designed all people so their gifts would work to benefit others. The problem is, many people don't care two cents about anybody else. They use whatever talents they've got to make a better life for themselves. I hope you won't see things that way. Let Me help you discover your gifts and show you how to share them. You are gifted for a reason!

Your Creator,
>God

== == ==   == == == == == == == == ==

IF YOU REALLY LOOK, YOU'LL FIND ME

You will seek me and find me when you seek me with all your heart.

Jeremiah 29:13

Dear Child of Mine,

>Have you ever lost something that you didn't really expect to find again? Sure, you rummaged around the house looking for it, but since you didn't actually think you'd ever find it, you didn't really look with much hope or expectation. You know what happens in those situations? Since you don't expect to find it, you rarely do.

Some people look for Me like that. "Oh, God's out there, but He's so far above me, I'll never reach Him." Believe Me when I say that if you'll put your heart into looking for Me, you will find Me! I am so close to you. Open the eyes of your heart and really look. Expect Me to be here, because here I am.

Your Friend,
>God

== == ==   == == == == == == == == ==

I'LL NEVER GIVE UP ON YOU

For I am convinced that neither death nor life,
neither angels nor demons, neither the present
nor the future, nor any powers, neither height nor depth,
nor anything else in all creation, will be able to separate us
from the love of God that is in Christ Jesus our Lord.

Romans **8:38–39**

My Child,

>Have you ever thought that your good behavior could make Me love you more, or that your bad behavior could make Me love you less? You're not that powerful.

I already love you 100 percent! Your good behavior won't change that. And no matter how bad you are, I'll never stop loving you. Never! I sent My Son, Jesus, to endure an awful death so that you could be with Me. I chose you and bought you at a great price—the price of My own Son's life.

There's no mistake you can make that will cause Me to say, "That's it! I don't love you anymore!" You may give up on Me, but I'll never give up on you. I love you with a fierce love that knows no end.

Your Faithful Father,
>God

== == ==   == == == == == == == == ==

YOU ARE VERY GOOD

**God saw all that he had made,
and it was very good.**

Genesis 1:31

Dear Child of Mine,

>When I created this world, I looked around at everything I had made and said, "This is very good!" You are part of what I made, so you are a part of what I call "good." In fact, of all My creation, I'm most proud of you. Why? You were made in My image. You're like Me.

I put a lot of thought, creativity, and love into making you who you are. I have a plan and a purpose for your life. Even when you blow it, I still love you. You can make a mistake, but that doesn't make *you* a mistake. So whenever you fall down, just know that I can pick you up and start you over. You are "very good!"

Your Loving Creator,
>God

== == ==   == == == == == == == == ==

LISTEN TO THE SONG I WROTE ABOUT YOU

The Lord your God is with you, he is mighty to save.
He will take great delight in you,
he will quiet you with his love,
he will rejoice over you with singing.

| Zephaniah | 3:17 |

My Child,

>Have you ever thought about the fact that I like you? I don't just love you in some serious, religious way. I actually *like* you.

Have you ever seen a proud, first-time father with his toddler in the grocery store? That kid could be throwing all of the groceries out of the cart, and the dad's got this look on his face like, "That's my kid! Isn't he great!"

That's the way I feel about you. I'm showing you off to the angels up here. "Look! See My child! What a kid!" I sing songs to celebrate your life. You are My favorite, and don't let anybody tell you otherwise.

Your Biggest Fan,
>God

== == ==   == == == == == == == == ==

I WANT IT TO BE YOUR CHOICE

**But if serving the LORD seems undesirable to you,
then choose for yourselves this day
whom you will serve. . . .
But as for Me and my household,
we will serve the LORD.**

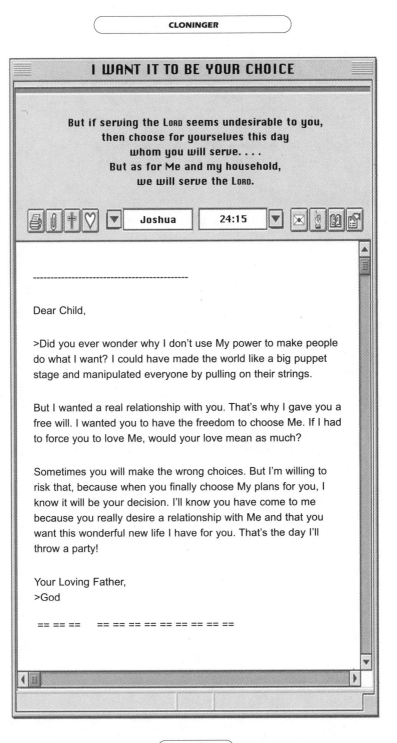

| | Joshua | 24:15 | |

Dear Child,

>Did you ever wonder why I don't use My power to make people do what I want? I could have made the world like a big puppet stage and manipulated everyone by pulling on their strings.

But I wanted a real relationship with you. That's why I gave you a free will. I wanted you to have the freedom to choose Me. If I had to force you to love Me, would your love mean as much?

Sometimes you will make the wrong choices. But I'm willing to risk that, because when you finally choose My plans for you, I know it will be your decision. I'll know you have come to me because you really desire a relationship with Me and that you want this wonderful new life I have for you. That's the day I'll throw a party!

Your Loving Father,
>God

I'M NOT THE OLD MAN UPSTAIRS

Surely the arm of the Lord is not too short
to save, nor his ear too dull to hear.

Isaiah | 59:1

Dear Child,

>When you think of Me, do you think of your grandfather? I'm
pretty old, so lots of people think of Me as an old human being.
I'm not. I sent My Son, Jesus, to show you My character.

Jesus was bold and strong—a carpenter from the age of twelve
until thirty. After He entered His ministry, He defeated demons,
He calmed a storm, and He turned over the tables of the money-
changers in the Temple.

Think about Me as Jesus' Father; I created the whole world. I
defeated entire armies with a wave of My hand. If you think I'm
weak or deaf, you've got the wrong God, my friend. I hear you,
and I am just waiting to help you. Call out to Me. I'm not your
grandfather or your great-grandfather. I'm your Father, the Ruler
of the universe. And I've got the power.

Your Heavenly Father,
>God

== == ==   == == == == == == == == ==

I TURN ON THE LIGHTS

God is light; in him there is no darkness at all.

1 John   1:5

Dear Child,

>Have you ever walked into a bright kitchen and seen a patch of darkness floating in the middle of the room? Probably not. Light drives out darkness. It can't be dark and light in the same place at the same time.

Now think about light as goodness and darkness as evil. My Son, Jesus, is the brightest light ever. On earth, He walked through some of the darkest, most evil places in the world. And everywhere He went, Jesus turned on the lights. Once He met a man who was blind, literally surrounded by darkness, and Jesus restored his sight.

My Son wants to shine in your life, too. Just ask Him, and Jesus will drive out the darkness around you. Hey, that's what He does!

The Illuminator,
>God

== == ==   == == == == == == == == ==

THERE ARE CLUES ALL AROUND YOU

I'm single-minded in pursuit of you; don't let me miss the road signs you've posted.

🖨 📎 ✝ ♡ ▼	Psalm 119:10	THE MESSAGE	▼	⊠ ✍ 📖 📋

My Child,

>I have posted obvious signs along your path that lead to Me. Keep your eyes open—there is no way that you're going to miss Me. I want you to find Me even more than you do. I've made the way clear and straight for those who are really looking.

There are clues all around you—in the outrageously beautiful world I made—in the diversity of people I created—in their millions of different fingerprints and individual faces, voices, and personalities. Best of all, I planted clues inside of your own heart—a soft voice that tells you with every beat that I am real, and I love you. Follow the clues.

Your Loving Father,
>God

== == ==   == == == == == == == == ==

YOU DON'T HAVE TO PROVE ANYTHING

Don't try to get into the good graces of
important people, but enjoy the company of
ordinary folks. And don't think you know it all!

Romans | **12:16 TLB**

My Child,

>You don't have to prove to other people how cool or popular you are, or elbow your way into the "in" crowd by pretending to be something you're not. Believe Me, you are a treasure to Me just because you're you.

It's your inner self that makes you valuable. I want you to learn to value yourself. You'll never be happy until you do. It doesn't matter how many "big shots" you impress, if you still hate yourself inside, you're going to be miserable. Find your worth in our relationship.

Learn to enjoy all kinds of ordinary people without putting on any kind of act. Each person is special and rare to Me—just as you are.

Your Creator,
>God

== == ==   == == == == == == == == ==

DON'T BE SCARED

Let us draw near to God with a sincere heart in full assurance of faith.

Hebrews	10:22

Dear Child of Mine,

>Have you ever stayed out past your curfew and then tried to sneak in? If your parents caught you, you probably felt ashamed.

A lot of people approach Me in the same way. They feel ashamed, so when they pray, it sounds something like this: "Oh, God, I know you hate me. I'm so rotten. You'll never forgive me." If you've done something wrong that you need to confess, tell Me. Get it over with, and then come to Me with assurance.

Don't be scared. I'm your heavenly Father. Because of what Jesus did on the cross, you can come to Me with confidence that I'll always receive you. I'll always forgive you. I know what you've done, and I love you anyway.

The One Who Accepts You,
>God

== == ==   == == == == == == == == ==

IT'S A JUNGLE OUT THERE!

**A righteous man may have many troubles,
but the LORD delivers him from them all.**

| | Psalm | 34:19 | |

Dear Child,

>People are so confused about the way I work. They think My job is to get rid of all their troubles. I'm supposed to fix every bad situation and make every circumstance perfect.

Sorry. That's not My job. I will fix many of your circumstances, but you're still going to have some troubles. The good news is, as you get to know Me, you'll find that I am always with you. I will lead you through your troubles and out the other side.

Think of your life as a jungle, and I'm your Guide. I'm not going to turn the whole jungle into Disneyland. But I will lead you *through* the jungle. When your life gets wild, don't freak out. Just stick close. I'll get you through it.

Your Guide,
>God

== == ==   == == == == == == == == ==

MY OPERATING INSTRUCTIONS

I tell you the truth, whoever hears my word and believes him who sent me has eternal life and will not be condemned; he has crossed over from death to life.

John 5:24

My Child,

>When you buy a new car, it comes with a little manual of operating instructions. That manual contains everything you need to know about taking care of your new automobile—what kind of gasoline is recommended, how often it will need servicing, and how much air pressure to put in your tires.

The words in the operator's manual are the link between the manufacturer and the car owner, and the extent to which the owner acts on those words will determine the performance of the car.

You get it, don't you? I made you. You are My creation. I am, in effect, the manufacturer of your life. But I have taken the risk of putting you into your own hands. My words for the care of My wonderful creation (you) are found in the Bible. Those words are life-giving. Read, believe, and take action.

Your Father,
>God

== == ==   == == == == == == == == ==

GOD DON'T MAKE NO JUNK

**As for God, his way is perfect;
the word of the LORD is flawless.**

| Psalm | 18:30 |

Dear Child,

>You grow up expecting your parents to be perfect, and when you first realize that they're not, it's disappointing. After all, you trusted them. They taught you everything. They had all the answers.

But as the saying goes, "nobody's perfect"—except Me. I have never made a mistake, and I never will. Do you think giraffes were a mistake? Think again. I made them, and I'm perfect. Everything I do and say is perfect.

Do you think you're a mistake? No way! Remember, I don't make mistakes. I made you exactly the way you are for a reason. Stick with Me, and I'll show you why I'm so proud of you.

Your Creator,
>God

== == ==   == == == == == == == == ==

I KNOW WHAT WILL MAKE YOU HAPPY

It is obvious what kind of life develops out of trying
to get your own way all the time: . . . loveless, cheap sex;
a stinking accumulation of mental and emotional garbage;
frenzied and joyless grabs for happiness; trinket gods;
. . . uncontrolled and uncontrollable addictions.

Galatians | **5:19-21 THE MESSAGE**

My Child,

>The reason I don't want you to live a self-centered, self-seeking
life is not because I'm a party pooper or an old meanie. It's
because living like that will make you miserable. Guaranteed.

A lifetime of putting yourself at the center of your own universe
will turn you into a caricature of low ideals and degrading habits.
It will sink you into the mire of competition, trap you in a cycle of
never-satisfied desires, and steal from you the joys of simple
serenity.

I made you, and I know what will make you happy. You were
designed to love other people and Me. That's where your
happiness lies—not in an endless chase after selfish pleasures.
Take My Word for it.

Your Heavenly Father,
>God

== == ==   == == == == == == == == ==

I'M FUN

Delight yourself in the LORD and he will
give you the desires of your heart.

Psalm **37:4**

Dear Child,

>Most people want a lot of "stuff" because they think it will make them happy. Think about it. You don't want a boat just to have a boat; you want a boat because of the fun you can have in it.

That's why some rich people who don't know Me keep buying more stuff. They think their possessions will make them happy, but it never works. If you spend time with Me, you'll find out that what you really want is a relationship with Me. I made you to need Me, and until you know Me, you won't really be happy.

Get to know Me, and I'll satisfy your desires. (I may even throw in a boat, too! You never can tell.)

The Joy-Giver,
>God

== == ==   == == == == == == == == ==

USE YOUR GIFTS CREATIVELY

Make a careful exploration of who you are and the work you have been given, and then sink yourself into that. Don't be impressed with yourself. Don't compare yourself with others. Each of you must take responsibility for doing the creative best you can with your own life.

Galatians | 6:4-5 THE MESSAGE

My Child,

>I guess you've noticed that I didn't crank out a world of clones. Even if you looked in every city and town on the planet, you would never find another person exactly like you. You are an original, inside and out.

Part of your assignment as My child is to get to know yourself—what you're good at and what you like. This isn't a competition between you and anyone else. I don't grade on the curve. Be confident—you have a right to be. You're awesome!

Let Me help you discover how to use the gifts I've given you, performing work that you find exciting. I want to see your life count for something great!

Your Creator,
>God

== == ==   == == == == == == == == ==

I'M ALL FOR YOU

**What, then, shall we say in response to this?
If God is for us, who can be against us?**

| Romans | 8:31 |

My Child,

>Does it ever seem like your whole life is one great big contest?
Or like every person you meet is grading you? Other kids are
checking you out, sizing up your looks, your clothes, your
personality, and your "cool factor." Teachers are grading your test
papers with their red markers, ready to make a nasty slash
across the slightest error. Parents are on to you about
homework, curfews, and keeping your room clean.

Well, I want you to know that I'm for you, now and forever. So no
matter what kind of "grade" you're getting with anyone else, you
can walk around with this quiet, confident secret inside: "God is
on my side."

Your Father and Friend,
>God

== == ==   == == == == == == == == ==

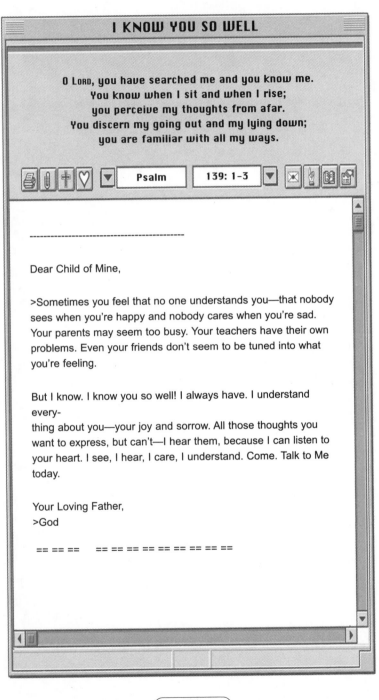

I KNOW YOU SO WELL

O Lord, you have searched me and you know me.
You know when I sit and when I rise;
you perceive my thoughts from afar.
You discern my going out and my lying down;
you are familiar with all my ways.

Psalm **139: 1-3**

Dear Child of Mine,

>Sometimes you feel that no one understands you—that nobody sees when you're happy and nobody cares when you're sad. Your parents may seem too busy. Your teachers have their own problems. Even your friends don't seem to be tuned into what you're feeling.

But I know. I know you so well! I always have. I understand every-
thing about you—your joy and sorrow. All those thoughts you want to express, but can't—I hear them, because I can listen to your heart. I see, I hear, I care, I understand. Come. Talk to Me today.

Your Loving Father,
>God

== == ==   == == == == == == == == ==

DON'T BE AFRAID

Say to those with fearful hearts, "Be strong, do not fear; your God will come, he will come with vengeance; with divine retribution he will come to save you."

Isaiah **35:4**

My Child,

>Sometimes you've wondered where I am. You've said, "Doesn't God see what I'm going through? Where is He?"

I want you to know that I do care about you, and I am here to rescue you. This world can be a scary place, but I am in control. If someone is frightening you—a relative, a teacher, or a bully— pray to Me. Ask Me for help. I am the Father of the fatherless. That means if there's no one there to protect you, then it's My job to protect you. Hang in there! I'm on My way.

Your Protector,
>God

== == ==   == == == == == == == == ==

LISTEN TO THE WORLD AROUND YOU

The heavens declare the glory of God;
the skies proclaim the work of his hands.

Psalm **19:1**

My Child,

>Who do you think paints the sunsets? Do you think they just happen? Who do you think made the deep blue sky and the towering pine trees? Did they just "bang" into existence?

No picture paints itself. No building builds itself. So why would the world be any different? I made the earth and everything in it. Every blade of grass points to Me—the Creator. Every waterfall thunders My signature. Open your eyes and look around you. Creation didn't just happen by chance. I made it all.

And the greatest part of My creation is you. Take time to observe and enjoy the world I made, and before long, you will see My hand in all of it. I am the Author of it all.

The Creator,
>God

== == ==   == == == == == == == == ==

MIRACLES ARE STILL MY BUSINESS

**You are the God who performs miracles;
you display your power among the peoples.**

| 🖨 📎 ✝ ♡ ▼ | Psalm | 77:14 | ▼ ✉ 🤚 📖 📋 |

My Child,

>Some people are looking for a big show of power from Me. Some think that if they could just see a miracle or two, they'd jump on the bandwagon and believe in Me. Well, plenty of people saw Jesus perform miracles when He was on earth. Some accepted Him, and some didn't. It's all a matter of what you choose to believe.

You are surrounded by miracles every day. Every time a flower blooms, it's a miracle. Every time a baby takes its first steps, or every time a husband and wife forgive one another, it's a miracle. I still do inexplicable and wonderful things every day—like multiplying food for the hungry and healing the sick. So keep your eyes open and choose to believe. Miracles are still My business!

The Miracle-Maker,
>God

== == ==   == == == == == == == == ==

I GIVE GOOD GIFTS

Which of you, if his son asks for bread, will give him a stone? Or if he asks for a fish, will give him a snake? If you, then, though you are evil, know how to give good gifts to your children, how much more will your Father in heaven give good gifts to those who ask him!

| Matthew | 7: 9-11 |

My Child,

>Parents aren't perfect, and some of them aren't exactly role models, but they at least have sense enough to feed their kids bread instead of rocks!

But I am the perfect Father. That means every time you want to talk, I want to listen. Every time you want to cry, I want to hold you. Every time you need advice, I want to give it. I know you can't see Me, but I am here. I celebrate your victories and grieve your losses. I write songs about you and sing them to you while you sleep. I brag on you to Jesus and the angels. I love you!

I give good gifts, so ask Me for what you need. I will never ignore or hurt you. I am so proud of you!

Your Loving Father,
>God

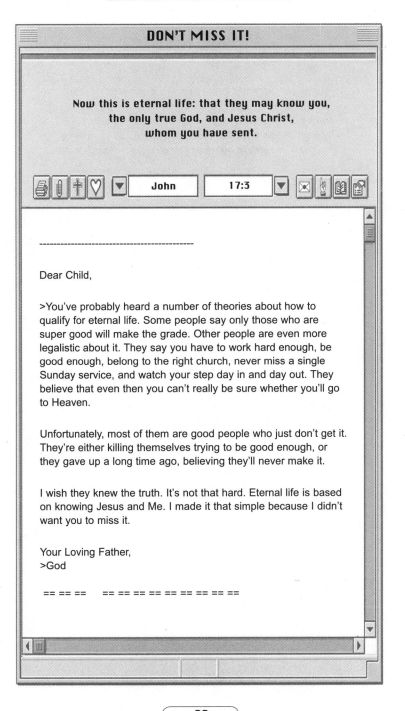

DON'T MISS IT!

Now this is eternal life: that they may know you, the only true God, and Jesus Christ, whom you have sent.

John   17:3

Dear Child,

>You've probably heard a number of theories about how to qualify for eternal life. Some people say only those who are super good will make the grade. Other people are even more legalistic about it. They say you have to work hard enough, be good enough, belong to the right church, never miss a single Sunday service, and watch your step day in and day out. They believe that even then you can't really be sure whether you'll go to Heaven.

Unfortunately, most of them are good people who just don't get it. They're either killing themselves trying to be good enough, or they gave up a long time ago, believing they'll never make it.

I wish they knew the truth. It's not that hard. Eternal life is based on knowing Jesus and Me. I made it that simple because I didn't want you to miss it.

Your Loving Father,
>God

I CALL YOU BY NAME

"Woman," he said, "why are you crying? Who is it
you are looking for?" Thinking he was the gardener,
she said, "Sir, if you have carried him away, tell me
where you have put him. . . ." Jesus said to her, "Mary."
She turned toward him and cried out . . . "Teacher."

| | John | 20:15-16 | |

My Child,

>At school, have you ever been lined up by number instead of
by name? Pretty impersonal, isn't it? Driver's license numbers,
credit card numbers, and Social Security numbers are part of
your everyday life.

It's so different when you hear your name spoken by someone
you love! When Mary went to the tomb after the crucifixion, she
found it empty and began to cry. But moments later, a familiar
voice spoke one simple word, "Mary." Just hearing Him say her
name, Mary knew Jesus was alive!

Listen for My voice. When I speak your name, you'll know that
I'm alive in your life, too. You will never be a number to Me.

Love,
>God

== == ==   == == == == == == == == ==

CAN'T GET NO SATISFACTION?

Jesus answered, "Everyone who drinks this
water will be thirsty again, but whoever drinks
the water I give him will never thirst."

John | 4:13-14

Dear Child,

>In the Middle East during Jesus' lifetime, there was no running
water. People had to draw their water from community wells.

One day, Jesus met a woman who had walked a long way from
her house in town just to draw water from one of those wells.
When Jesus told her that one drink of His special water would
satisfy her thirst forever, it got her attention. To her, His promise
meant she was free from her daily trip to the well. She didn't
realize at first that Jesus was speaking of a spiritual principle. He
promised her living water, and that's what I'm promising you.

I built you with a thirst for Me that only My Son, Jesus, can
satisfy. The dirty well water of this world will never satisfy you.
Turn on the faucet of Jesus in your heart. His love is a like a cold
drink—it satisfies!

Your Father,
>God

== == ==   == == == == == == == == ==

FRIENDSHIP IS A TWO-WAY STREET

I say: My purpose will stand, and I will do all that I please. . . . What I have said, that will I bring about; what I have planned, that will I do.

| Isaiah | 46:10-11 |

Dear Child,

>Do you realize that I've existed forever, and I will always exist? I'm not just some illusion that you've dreamed up. I really do exist. Even when you turn on the television set or party with your friends, I'm still with you. You just can't hear Me then, because you're not paying any attention to Me.

I want you to get to know Me, but if you don't spend time with Me, how will you know My voice? Friendship is a two-way street. I love you and will always love you, but if you don't spend time with Me, how can you think of Me as a friend? I want to spend time with you. But it's your choice. I choose to love you whatever you do.

Your Father,
>God

== == ==   == == == == == == == == ==

YOUR SPIRIT WILL AGREE WITH MINE

God's Spirit touches our spirits and confirms who we really are. We know who he is, and we know who we are: Father and children.

Romans 8:16 | THE MESSAGE

Dear Child,

>I communicate through My Spirit. I know that's hard to understand. But My Spirit is communicating something majorly important to you right now. My Spirit is telling you Who I am. He's telling you who you are and Whose you are: I am your Father. You are My child.

It's so important for you to know and believe this. Check it out for yourself. If you turn down all the other noises in your life—the TV, CD player, and your computer video games—and get alone with Me, you'll know what My Spirit is saying: "Your Father loves you! Trust and believe."

Love,
>God

== == ==   == == == == == == == == ==

THE BIBLE IS NOT A FAD

**Heaven and earth will pass away, but
my words will never pass away.**

| Matthew | 24:35 |

Dear Child of Mine,

>Your world is changing. To you, e-mail is new. To your great-grandparents, the telephone was new. To your great-great-great grandparents, "snail mail" was new.

As new things develop, old things pass away. All governments eventually fail. Even the earth and the sky will one day disappear. But My words in the Bible will never change. They always have and always will be true. They are just as relevant for you as they were for someone a thousand years ago. Circumstances may change, but truth is always truth.

If you are relying on a new fad, a new drug, a new president, or some new technology to make you happy, you're going to be disappointed. But if you rely on the Bible to guide your life, you will never go wrong. My Word doesn't change. You can count on it.

Your Everlasting Father,
>God

== == ==   == == == == == == == == ==

CLUB BEVERLY HILLS?

Dear friends, do not be surprised at the painful trial you are suffering, as though something strange were happening to you.

I Peter 4:12

My Child,

>Have you ever felt ripped-off or cheated about some little thing, and then felt ashamed because you saw starving kids on the news who had it a lot worse than you? It kind of puts things in perspective, doesn't it? Everyone has trouble, including Christians. So rather than complaining, ask Me, "What do you want me to get out of this experience?" Maybe you're suffering because of something you shouldn't have done. Ask, and I'll show you what it is.

But sometimes, if you are a follower of Jesus, you might suffer persecution just for who you are. Can you still trust that I'm in control? If you look at this world as a training camp, it's not such a bad place. But if you expect to spend your life at a country club, you're going to be one whiny camper. Everybody hurts sometimes. So hang in there.

Your Comforter,
>God

== == ==   == == == == == == == == ==

FREE STEAK DINNER

**[The Lord] brought me out into a spacious place;
he rescued me because he delighted in me.**

Psalm   18:19

My Child,

>Whenever I hear people say, "Oh, I'm doing pretty well under
the circumstances," I always want to say, "What are you doing
under the circumstances? Get out from under there!"

I want your life to be better than just okay. I want it to be
awesome! I know everybody has hard days sometimes. But My
point is that it will always get better. If you're starving, a peanut
butter and jelly sandwich tastes good, but a steak dinner tastes
even better. I want to rescue you from your situation. It may take
some time, but if you stick with Me, I'll lift you high above the
circumstances. I want to bless you.

Your Father of Abundance,
>God

== == ==   == == == == == == == == ==

HOW ABOUT A FRESH START?

**Count yourself lucky, how happy you must be—
You get a fresh start, your slate's wiped clean.**

Psalm 32:1 | THE MESSAGE

My Child,

>A lot of kids act like there's no right and wrong. They've got a "do whatever feels good" attitude. But when those same kids go against their consciences, I guarantee you, they feel guilty. They may not let you know about it, but they do. They try to stuff the guilt down deep inside and end up getting mad at Me. It nags at them, so some of them take pills or start drinking to drown out My voice.

The only real way to lose the guilt is by asking Me for forgiveness. I'm the only One Who can let you off the hook. The good news is, I can and will erase your wrong every time. You can start fresh, just as if it never happened. So if you feel guilty about some of the things you've done, bring them to Me. I'll always forgive you.

Your Best Friend,
>God

== == ==   == == == == == == == == ==

MAKE KNOWING ME YOUR GOAL

What is more, I consider everything a loss compared to the surpassing greatness of knowing Christ Jesus my Lord.

Philippians 3:8

My Child,

>It's one thing to know about someone, but it's a different thing to really know that person. For instance, you know about the President of the United States, but if you dropped by the White House today, you probably wouldn't get invited to lunch.

My child, Job, knew about Me. But after he had an encounter with Me, it was a whole different deal. The Apostle Paul's one goal in life was getting to know Jesus. In fact, he considered everything else a big pile of trash compared with that goal.

Maybe, like Job, you've heard about Me all your life. Maybe you can sing "Jesus Loves Me" with the best of them. But that doesn't mean you know Jesus or Me. To know Us is to enter into a relationship with Us. Make that your goal.

Your Friend,
>God

== == ==   == == == == == == == == ==

I WANT TO AMAZE YOU

Call to me and I will answer you and tell you great and unsearchable things you do not know.

Jeremiah 33:3

Dear Child of Mine,

>Part of the fun of being God is blowing people's minds. I'm serious! I know everything, and every now and then, I'll share something deep with one of My children. I love watching their eyes pop open as the light goes off in their heads and they say, "Wow, I get it!"

I have some of those eye-opening revelations that I want to share with you. I've created you to understand and appreciate things about Me that no one else will ever know. I want to share it with you and only you. Spend time with Me and call on Me. Read My Book. Then listen and prepare to be amazed.

Your Maker,
>God

== == ==   == == == == == == == == ==

THE GIFT OF CONTENTMENT

Keep your lives free from the love of money and be
content with what you have, because God has said,
"Never will I leave you; never will I forsake you."

Hebrews 13:5

Dear Child,

>Have you heard the battle cry of the world—"more, More,
MORE?" Have you seen the "troops" lining up outside the mall,
manned with their credit cards, ready to attack! Doors open . . .
ready . . . charge!

That army is always looking for recruits, but "more" will not buy
you happiness, whether it's more money or more stuff. But I
have a gift that *will* bring you happiness. It is the gift of
contentment. To be content is to feel glad about where you are
with what you have. Rich? Okay. Poor? Okay. Plain? Okay.
Fancy? Okay. To be content is to take your eyes off of money
and stuff and turn them on Me. Let Me shower you with the
riches of My love.

Your Source,
>God

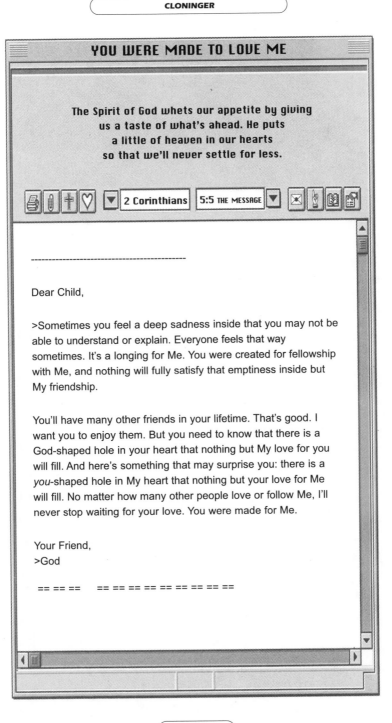

YOU WERE MADE TO LOVE ME

The Spirit of God whets our appetite by giving
us a taste of what's ahead. He puts
a little of heaven in our hearts
so that we'll never settle for less.

2 Corinthians 5:5 THE MESSAGE

Dear Child,

>Sometimes you feel a deep sadness inside that you may not be able to understand or explain. Everyone feels that way sometimes. It's a longing for Me. You were created for fellowship with Me, and nothing will fully satisfy that emptiness inside but My friendship.

You'll have many other friends in your lifetime. That's good. I want you to enjoy them. But you need to know that there is a God-shaped hole in your heart that nothing but My love for you will fill. And here's something that may surprise you: there is a *you*-shaped hole in My heart that nothing but your love for Me will fill. No matter how many other people love or follow Me, I'll never stop waiting for your love. You were made for Me.

Your Friend,
>God

== == ==   == == == == == == == == ==

WILL YOU LOVE MY WORLD WITH ME?

Dear friends, since God so loved us,
we also ought to love one another.

| 1 John | 4:11 |

Dear Child,

>In the beginning, My world was a little jewel of a planet with fields and forests full of amazing animals, waters full of fascinating fish, and skies full of glorious birds. But My masterpiece was the human family.

My plan for human beings was that they live forever in harmony with each other and Me. But they wanted their own way instead of Mine, so now there's a lot of sickness and sadness in My once-beautiful world.

Why don't I just wave a magic wand and fix it? Magic wands are not My thing. I work through people like you, who will love the lonely with My love and reach out to the broken with My touch. I need your heart to care, your hands to heal, your feet to go, and your voice to tell the truth. Will you love My world with Me?

Your Creator,
>God

== == ==   == == == == == == == == ==

MY PATH IS NARROW, BUT NOT THAT NARROW

**You broaden the path beneath me,
so that my ankles do not turn.**

Psalm 18:36

My Child,

>Grace is a word you need to understand. Grace is Me giving you more than you deserve. It's Me cutting you some slack.

Some people feel that obeying Me is like walking across Niagara Falls on a tightrope. One mistake—one wrong move—and down they go. But they've got it all wrong. I've built you a highway across Niagara Falls. Sure you'll make mistakes, but you'll never fall out of My grace. How will you ever learn to walk straight if I shoot you down for every single mistake you make? Trust Me. I'm not like that.

If you do the wrong thing, just ask for My forgiveness, get up, and try again. I am for you, not against you.

The Forgiver,
>God

MY SON'S LOVE IS A LIFEBOAT

**I tell you the truth,
he who believes has everlasting life.**

| | John | 6:47 | |

My Child,

>Long ago, a huge British ship called the *Titanic* was hit by an iceberg on its maiden voyage. The *Titanic* was considered man's unsinkable masterpiece, and yet it sank. Hundreds of lives were lost, drowned in the icy sea, because the ship was not prepared for the emergency. There were not enough life jackets or lifeboats for everyone aboard.

Everyone will face death sometime, but I have a life jacket for you. It is My truth. I have a lifeboat for you—it is the mercy and love of Jesus Christ. I will not make you put on the life jacket. I will not make you climb into the boat. But I have prepared them for you.

If you will wear the life jacket of My truth and climb into the lifeboat of My Son's mercy, you will live. Come on. Get into the boat!

Your Lifesaver,
>God

== == ==   == == == == == == == == ==

DON'T JUST HEAR, TAKE ACTION!

Do not merely listen to the word, and so deceive yourselves. Do what it says.

James 1:22

My Child,

>By now you should know I'm a take-action kind of God. And nothing would make Me happier than getting you in on the action. Here's how it works. When you feel Me nudging you to do something, don't fool around. Do it! When you sense Me giving you directions, follow them!

This is where the adventure begins. Listening for My voice and then doing what I say is exciting. It's a secret just between you and Me. But be sure of this: I will never contradict myself. I'll never tell you to do anything that goes against what the Bible says. I'll never tell you to do anything Jesus wouldn't have done. That's why it's important for you to read the Bible and know My Son.

Ready to try it? This is going to be fun!

Your Friend,
>God

== == ==   == == == == == == == == ==

IT'S OKAY TO START SMALL

Now he began teaching them again about the
Kingdom of God. "What is the Kingdom like?" he asked.
". . . It is like a tiny mustard seed planted in
a garden; soon it grows into a tall bush,
and the birds live among its branches."

| Luke | 13:18-19 TLB |

My Child,

>My kingdom is amazing and wonderful. It beats any magic
show you've ever seen! It begins in a person's life as a small
seed of faith—about the size of a sesame seed on a hamburger
bun. It looks so insignificant that nobody pays any attention to it
at all. Nobody but Me, that is.

My eyes are constantly on that seed of faith. I watch as it's
planted in the rich soil of My love and mercy. I am constantly
coaxing and urging and encouraging it to grow. Little by little and
bit by bit, your faith begins to bush out, develop branches, and
take on leaves. Then one day, people look in amazement at
you—a "beautiful tree," creating shade, safety, and beauty in My
world. Plant your faith in My love today.

Your Seed Sower,
>God

== == ==   == == == == == == == == ==

HAVE I GOT A PLAN FOR YOU!

"For I know the plans I have for you," declares
the LORD, "plans to prosper you and not to harm
you, plans to give you hope and a future."

Jeremiah   29: 11

My Child,

>Sometimes it seems like everyone, including your friends, your
parents, and maybe even yourself, has a plan for you. Well, I
have a plan for you, too. I created you with it in mind. It is your
destiny—the reason you exist.

We have adventures to go on, you and I. There are new friends
for you to meet and new places for you to explore. There will be
tough times, but I'll give you strength; and when you're lost, I'll
show you the way back home.

So when you need to make a decision, pray first and then listen.
You will hear My voice like a whisper inside yourself. Trust Me. I
only want to bless you.

Your Trail Guide,
>God

== == ==   == == == == == == == == ==

CHURCH IS COOL

**I love the house where you live, O Lord,
the place where your glory dwells.**

Psalm	26:8

Dear Child,

>I live with My children. Does that mean I live in a building? Well, when those who love Me and follow My Son, Jesus, are meeting in a building, I'm there, too. There's nothing I like better than to show up and be in the middle of things! But when they leave, I follow them home. Why would I want to hang around an empty building?

Wherever My people are, even when they're alone, that's where you'll find Me. But if you really want to see Me in action, go to one of their meetings where they praise and worship Me. Find a church full of happy, loving people who are excited about Me. It's a blast! See you there!

Your Faithful Father,
>God

== == ==   == == == == == == == == ==

BIGGER THAN THE BOOGEY MAN!

**The LORD is with me; I will not be afraid.
What can man do to me?**

| Psalm | 118:6 |

Dear Child,

>Have you ever been spooked while walking alone at night?
Maybe there was a noise in the bushes or a dog was barking,
and it just scared you.

Now what if you had been out walking with a friend? You probably
wouldn't even have noticed the barking dog. Things just aren't as
scary with a friend by your side, so let Me walk with you.

I am everywhere all the time, and that means I am with you
always. I am your best Friend. You are never alone.

So think about Me the next time that you're afraid. Let My
nearness dissolve your fear. You don't need to be frightened
anymore.

Your Best Friend,
>God

== == ==   == == == == == == == == ==

CHANGE STATIONS TODAY

**I can do everything through him
who gives me strength.**

[Philippians] [4:13]

Dear Child,

>Don't listen to that old radio station in your head that keeps singing yesterday's hit: "I can't, I can't, I can't." Change stations today! Tune into Me and get the sound of the truth going inside you.

The truth will sing a totally different song. The words go like this: *There's nothing you can't do! Anything and everything is possible. When you trust Me, I'll give you strength to see—there's absolutely nothing you can't do!*

Once you get hold of that powerful reality, you'll see locked doors fly open. You'll find solutions to problems that used to look hopeless. And you'll realize that it's Me working in you, strengthening you, and helping you do what needs doing. Tune into My truth today!

Your DJ,
>God

== == ==   == == == == == == == == ==

MY KIND OF PERSON

But Jesus called the children to him and said,
"Let the little children come to me, and
do not hinder them, for the kingdom
of God belongs to such as these."

Luke 18:16

Dear Child,

>Have you ever wondered who I like to hang out with most? You might think it would be kings or presidents—powerful people who call all the shots. Wrong! You might think it would be the most religious people—the ones who could make 100 on a Bible quiz. Wrong again. Maybe you'd guess sports stars or movie stars. No, not really. I'm not impressed with money or fame.

The people I love to spend time with are the ones with childlike hearts—the ones who are not always pushing into the spotlight, but who want to let somebody else shine. I have a heart for the ones who are willing to take a back seat and not act like know-it-alls—the ones who wait for My words and listen for My voice. Are you My kind of person?

Your Loving Father,
>God

== == ==   == == == == == == == == ==

I'LL BE THE JUDGE OF THAT!

You, therefore, have no excuse, you who pass
judgment on someone else, for at whatever
point you judge the other, you are
condemning yourself, because you
who pass judgment do the same things.

Romans **2:1**

Dear Child,

>Every time you start criticizing someone else, that criticism
boomerangs and comes around to hit you in the head. Every
time you act as judge and jury for someone else, you end up
putting a noose around your own neck. Every time you point
your index finger at someone else, look at your hand. There are
three other fingers pointing back at you.

Listen, there's only one Person on the judging committee, and
that's Me. I'm the only One Who can look inside a heart and see
its motives. I'm the only One Who can pour out grace undiluted
by prejudice. When you judge someone else, you just end up
judging yourself. So give other people the benefit of the doubt
and leave the judging to Me.

Your Father of Grace,
>God

== == ==   == == == == == == == == ==

PRESCRIPTION FOR A GOOD LIFE

**Whoeuer wants to embrace life and see the day
fill up with good, Here's what you do:
Say nothing euil or hurtful; Snub euil and
cultiuate good; run after peace for all you're worth.**

1 Peter | 3:18-11 THE MESSAGE

Dear Child,

>Want a prescription for a good life? I've got one, but don't
expect anything supernatural. It's plain old common sense. Here
it is: Don't run off at the mouth with harmful gossip and mindless
chatter. You can hurt other people with your words.

When you see your friends headed for trouble, turn around and
run in the other direction. It's not worth being part of the crowd if
the crowd is getting ready to throw itself off a cliff. It doesn't take
a rocket scientist to figure out that reckless, dangerous choices
lead to a reckless, dangerous life.

So run away from what's bad for you, and run after what's good.
You'll be rewarding yourself with peace and happiness, and your
regrets will be few. Trust Me!

The Author of Common Sense,
>God

== == ==   == == == == == == == == ==

I WILL BE CHEERING YOU ON

When you give to the needy, do not let your left
hand know what your right hand is doing,
so that your giving may be in secret. Then your Father,
who sees what is done in secret, will reward you.

Matthew 6:3-4

My Child,

>Jesus loved to see His followers doing good things for others,
but He warned them not to be show-offs about it. His warning is
still in effect.

It's not necessary to act super holy to impress other people. Be
quiet about the good things you do. It's more fun that way. Even if
no one else sees your good deeds, I'll notice. My eyes of love will
be on you. Your good deeds will be our secret—yours and Mine.

I'm watching and cheering you on and giving you the quiet
reward of My approval. I'm pulling for you!

Your Rewarder,
>God

== == ==   == == == == == == == == ==

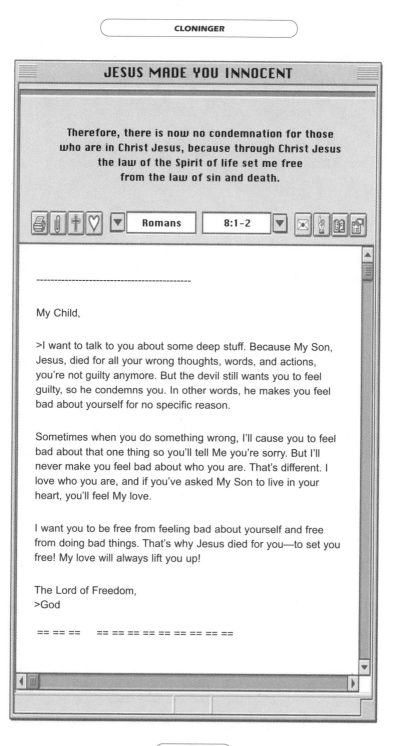

JESUS MADE YOU INNOCENT

Therefore, there is now no condemnation for those
who are in Christ Jesus, because through Christ Jesus
the law of the Spirit of life set me free
from the law of sin and death.

Romans 8:1-2

My Child,

>I want to talk to you about some deep stuff. Because My Son,
Jesus, died for all your wrong thoughts, words, and actions,
you're not guilty anymore. But the devil still wants you to feel
guilty, so he condemns you. In other words, he makes you feel
bad about yourself for no specific reason.

Sometimes when you do something wrong, I'll cause you to feel
bad about that one thing so you'll tell Me you're sorry. But I'll
never make you feel bad about who you are. That's different. I
love who you are, and if you've asked My Son to live in your
heart, you'll feel My love.

I want you to be free from feeling bad about yourself and free
from doing bad things. That's why Jesus died for you—to set you
free! My love will always lift you up!

The Lord of Freedom,
>God

== == ==   == == == == == == == == ==

WISDOM IS AS WISDOM DOES

**For wisdom is more precious than rubies,
and nothing you desire can compare with her.**

Proverbs 8:11

Dear Child,

>You know, there are people with genius IQ's that still can't make a friend or get a date? To be smart and to be wise are two different things. Wisdom is knowing Me and living like I'm in control. It's one of the most valuable and desirable traits to acquire.

In the movie, *Forrest Gump,* Forrest is kind of slow; but his mom loves and believes in him. She tells him, "Stupid is as stupid does." I agree. I'll go on to say, "Wisdom is as wisdom does." You don't have to make straight A's to be wise.

So how can a young person gain wisdom? Read My Bible, particularly the book of Proverbs. It will make you wiser than some of your teachers. Don't wait until you're old and gray to be wise. Seek wisdom now.

The Source of All Wisdom,
>God

== == ==   == == == == == == == == ==

WHAT DO YOU WANT ME TO DO FOR YOU?

"What do you want me to do for you?" Jesus
asked him. The blind man said, "Rabbi, I want to see."
"Go," said Jesus, "your faith has healed you."
Immediately he received his sight
and followed Jesus along the road.

Mark 10:51-52

Dear Child,

>My Son has good manners. He would never push His way into
your life, changing and rearranging everything, without your
permission. He waits to be invited in, and then He waits to hear
what you want.

"What do you want Me to do for you?" He asked a blind man,
and the blind man answered, "Rabbi, I want to see." This man
had enough faith to ask for what he wanted, so Jesus didn't fool
around. He answered the blind man's request immediately, and
the blind man regained his sight. And more than that, he began
to follow Jesus.

What do you want Jesus to do for you? Do you want to see
Him? Believe in Him? That's one request He wants to answer. All
you have to do is ask.

Your Father,
>God

WHO WILL I BE TO YOU?

"But what about you?" [Jesus] asked.
"Who do you say I am?" Simon Peter answered,
"You are the Christ, the Son of the living God."

| Matthew | 16:15-16 |

My Dear Child,

>I'm not a gray-haired old geezer, sitting on a rusty throne in Heaven. I'm alive! I'm a powerful, present-tense Person, who loves you with a powerful, present-tense love. I was, and I am, and I will be forever. I am the unchanging Word of truth.

I can tell you Who I am. But only you can say Who I will be to you. I want to be your Father (a good Father Who's involved in your everyday life), your Friend (a Friend Who knows your strengths and weaknesses and is always on your side), your Savior (the One Who comes to your rescue in everyday problems), and your Guide through the tricky maze of life. It's your call. Who do you say that I am?

The Great I Am,
>God

== == == == == == == == == == ==

YOU CAN BE REAL WITH ME

There is a friend who sticks closer than a brother.

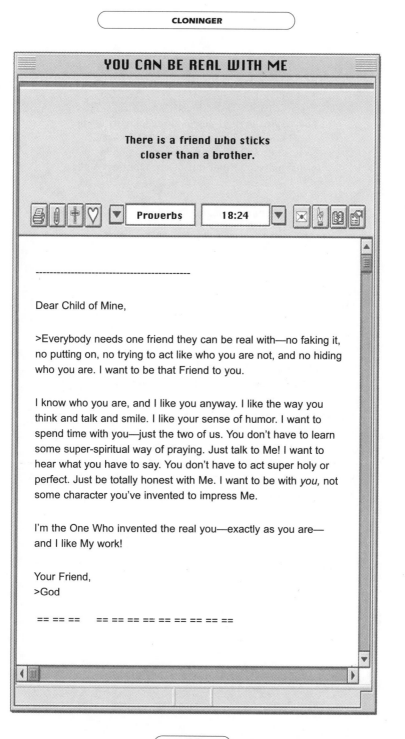

| Proverbs | 18:24 |

Dear Child of Mine,

>Everybody needs one friend they can be real with—no faking it, no putting on, no trying to act like who you are not, and no hiding who you are. I want to be that Friend to you.

I know who you are, and I like you anyway. I like the way you think and talk and smile. I like your sense of humor. I want to spend time with you—just the two of us. You don't have to learn some super-spiritual way of praying. Just talk to Me! I want to hear what you have to say. You don't have to act super holy or perfect. Just be totally honest with Me. I want to be with *you,* not some character you've invented to impress Me.

I'm the One Who invented the real you—exactly as you are—and I like My work!

Your Friend,
>God

== == ==   == == == == == == == == ==

DIVE INTO PRAYER

God's Spirit is right alongside helping us along.
If we don't know how or what to pray,
it doesn't matter. He does our praying in and
for us, making prayer out of our wordless sighs.

Romans 8:26 | THE MESSAGE

My Child,

>Prayer is an ongoing adventure. Dive into it like you would a deep, clear river and swim! Don't worry about knowing how to pray. My Spirit will be there to keep you afloat. He is the ultimate prayer partner. He prays with you, in you, and for you.

Sometimes you'll have a nagging feeling that there's something you need to pray about, but you can't seem to put your finger on what it is. That's when My Spirit goes into action. He sees what's in your heart—all those things you can't put into words—then He turns your sighs into prayers. And even though you may not know exactly what He's praying through you, I will know. And I will answer.

Your Prayer Partner,
>God

== == ==   == == == == == == == == ==

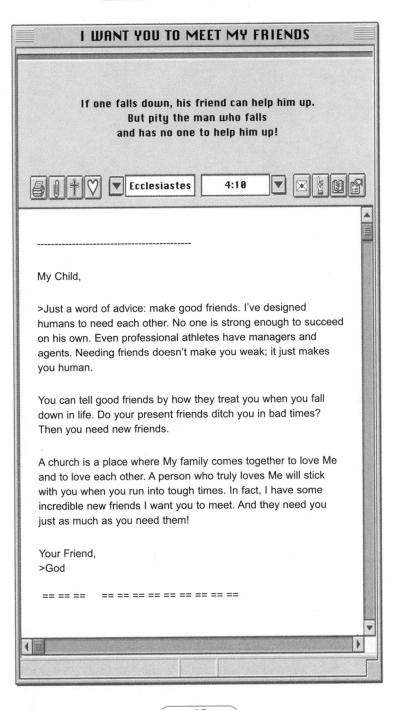

I WANT YOU TO MEET MY FRIENDS

If one falls down, his friend can help him up.
But pity the man who falls
and has no one to help him up!

Ecclesiastes 4:10

My Child,

>Just a word of advice: make good friends. I've designed
humans to need each other. No one is strong enough to succeed
on his own. Even professional athletes have managers and
agents. Needing friends doesn't make you weak; it just makes
you human.

You can tell good friends by how they treat you when you fall
down in life. Do your present friends ditch you in bad times?
Then you need new friends.

A church is a place where My family comes together to love Me
and to love each other. A person who truly loves Me will stick
with you when you run into tough times. In fact, I have some
incredible new friends I want you to meet. And they need you
just as much as you need them!

Your Friend,
>God

== == ==   == == == == == == == == ==

IT'S MY WORLD

Every animal of the forest is mine, and the cattle
on a thousand hills. I know every bird in the mountains,
and the creatures of the field are mine . . .
the world is mine, and all that is in it.

Psalm 50:10-12

My Child,

>The earth is mine, and I created everything in it. I personally
made every single atom in the universe! And I own everything,
even the things you think you own.

The reason I ask you to give your time and money to Me is that
it proves to both of us that you love Me more than you love what
I can give you. I know what your priorities are by how you spend
your time and money. Do you know what comes first in your life?

The good news for you is that I love you, and I will take care of
you. You don't need to worry about going broke. Your Father
owns everything!

The Creator,
>God

== == ==   == == == == == == == == ==

THE BEST FOOD IS FREE

**Come, all you who are thirsty, come to the waters;
and you who have no money, come, buy and eat!
Come, buy wine and milk without money and without
cost. Why spend money on what is not bread,
and your labor on what does not satisfy?**

| Isaiah | 55:1-2 |

Dear Child,

>A lot of people think that becoming a child of God requires following a bunch of impossible religious rules. "Yeah," they grumble, "I would live for God, but He doesn't want me. I can't be good enough anyway." *What a lie!*

Most free stuff is crummy. But My free gift of Heaven, where you will live in joy for eternity, is the most valuable present you'll ever receive. All you have to do to get to Heaven is to believe in and follow My Son, Jesus. And to have My power in your life, you just need to let Jesus sit in the driver's seat and take control of your life. That's it! Simple, isn't it?

Stop buying the moldy bread of this world, and come feast on My love for you. It's free!

Your Host,
>God

IT GETS BETTER, I PROMISE

**Weeping may remain for a night,
but rejoicing comes in the morning.**

Psalm	30:5

Dear Child,

>Unfortunately, sadness is sometimes a part of life on earth. I didn't create the world that way, but when men turned against Me, the world took a turn for the worse.

So there will be some times in your life when you are just plain sad. Jesus' friends were sad when He died; but then He came back to life, and they had a party. I work that way a lot. Sometimes things get worse before they really get better.

So when you're sad, just hang in there. In time, your sadness will lift. Even Jesus was sad. But He laughed and smiled a lot more than He cried. There may be some sad parts to the movie of life, but it has a happy ending. I promise.

The Creator of New Life,
>God

== == ==   == == == == == == == == ==

LET'S GET TO KNOW EACH OTHER BETTER

In your presence is fullness of joy; At your right hand are pleasures forevermore.

Psalm 16:11 NKJV

Dear Child,

>Have you ever had a crush on somebody? You know how it is; every time that person walks into the room, you get excited. If that person sits near you or talks to you, there's nowhere else that you would rather be. If that person goes to a party, you want to be there.

That's what I want our relationship to be like. I'm a person. I have a personality. As you begin to know Me better, you'll see. There's nothing in the world like being in My presence. As you set aside time to be alone with Me, expect it to be exciting. There are personal things I want to tell you. There are plans I want to share with you. I want to know you better. And I want you to know the joy of knowing Me. So let's spend time together!

Your Best Friend,
>God

== == ==   == == == == == == == == ==

LIVE CAREFREE!

**Live carefree before God;
he is most careful with you.**

| 1 Peter 5:7 | THE MESSAGE |

My Child,

>Is your life filled with worry? Do you find yourself getting stressed out over everything from tomorrow's English assignment to the price of chewing gum? That's no way for anyone to live, much less one of My children. I want you to wake up every morning feeling carefree, knowing the happiness that comes naturally to the child of a loving parent.

Have you ever noticed how babies in the arms of their mothers will sometimes throw themselves backwards, certain they will be caught? Or how toddlers jump from a high place into the waiting arms of their fathers, never doubting they'll be caught? That's the kind of carefree trust I want you to have in Me. Don't worry. Be happy!

Your Joy-Filled Father,
>God

== == ==   == == == == == == == == ==

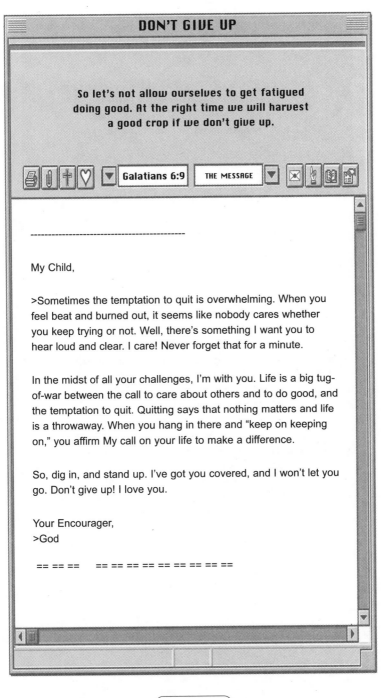

DON'T GIVE UP

So let's not allow ourselves to get fatigued
doing good. At the right time we will harvest
a good crop if we don't give up.

Galatians 6:9 | THE MESSAGE

My Child,

>Sometimes the temptation to quit is overwhelming. When you
feel beat and burned out, it seems like nobody cares whether
you keep trying or not. Well, there's something I want you to
hear loud and clear. I care! Never forget that for a minute.

In the midst of all your challenges, I'm with you. Life is a big tug-
of-war between the call to care about others and to do good, and
the temptation to quit. Quitting says that nothing matters and life
is a throwaway. When you hang in there and "keep on keeping
on," you affirm My call on your life to make a difference.

So, dig in, and stand up. I've got you covered, and I won't let you
go. Don't give up! I love you.

Your Encourager,
>God

SAY "YES" TO LIFE

But he took [the dead girl] by the hand and said,
"My child, get up!" Her spirit returned,
and at once she stood up. Then Jesus
told them to give her something to eat.

Luke   8:54-55

Dear Child,

>Sometimes the hardest thing in the world is not facing some big, heroic challenge. Sometimes the hardest thing is just getting up, getting dressed, and saying "yes" to life.

Eating breakfast, brushing your teeth, and putting one foot in front of the other is difficult when you want to pull the covers back over your head. It's easy to get discouraged and start feeling down on yourself or down on life.

On days like that, I want you to remember how much I believe in you. On days like that, I want you to hear My Son, Jesus, saying to you, "Get up! It's a new day, and I'll be with you in the midst of everything." If His love was powerful enough to raise a dead girl to life, don't you think it's powerful enough to give you the hope and energy you need for today? Say "yes" to life.

Your Life-Giver,
>God

== == ==   == == == == == == == == ==

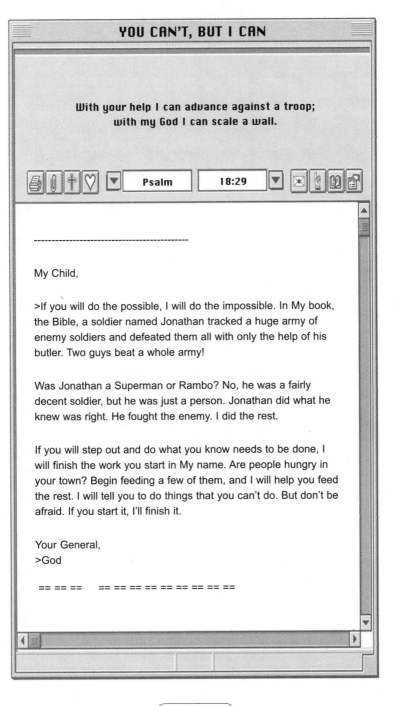

YOU CAN'T, BUT I CAN

With your help I can advance against a troop; with my God I can scale a wall.

Psalm 18:29

My Child,

>If you will do the possible, I will do the impossible. In My book, the Bible, a soldier named Jonathan tracked a huge army of enemy soldiers and defeated them all with only the help of his butler. Two guys beat a whole army!

Was Jonathan a Superman or Rambo? No, he was a fairly decent soldier, but he was just a person. Jonathan did what he knew was right. He fought the enemy. I did the rest.

If you will step out and do what you know needs to be done, I will finish the work you start in My name. Are people hungry in your town? Begin feeding a few of them, and I will help you feed the rest. I will tell you to do things that you can't do. But don't be afraid. If you start it, I'll finish it.

Your General,
>God

== == ==   == == == == == == == == ==

WHO ELSE IS LIKE ME?

There is no one like you, O Lord, and there is no God but you.

| 1 Chronicles | 17:20 |

Dear Child,

>I guarantee that you've never met anyone else like Me. I'm not bragging; it's just the truth.

Haven't I always forgiven you when you asked? Does anyone else know every thought you think and every dream you dream? Do you know anyone else who wants to be with you twenty-four hours a day? Has anyone else ever created a whole, beautiful world for you to live in, or created the air you breathe? Does anyone else have an exciting purpose for your life? Do you know anyone else who has prepared a home for you in Heaven, where you will never fear or hurt again?

I am the only One Who loves you in this way, and I want to share your life with you.

The One and Only,
>God

== == ==   == == == == == == == == ==

THIS IS NOT A SECRET CLUB

I have called you friends, for everything that I learned from my Father I have made known to you.

John | 15:15

Dear Child,

>When people talk behind your back, don't you hate it? It's like they're saying, "Oh, it's an inside joke; YOU wouldn't get it." There's nothing worse than being left out of a group when you want to fit in.

Here's good news: Jesus won't ever keep secrets from you. He came to earth so He could tell you every single thing about Me. He came to tell you about Heaven. He came to share My love with you.

Christianity is not some secret, exclusive club. All you have to do is want to join, and you're in. I've chosen you to belong. I sent My Son to invite you. Come and hang out with Us!

Your Friend,
>God

== == ==   == == == == == == == == ==

RUN AWAY! RUN AWAY!

**The name of the LORD is a strong tower;
the righteous run to it and are safe.**

| | Proverbs | 18:10 | |

My Child,

>Where do the good guys run to in the movies when the enemy storms the castle? The knights pull up the drawbridge, retreat into the inner tower, and wait it out. When your enemy is on your case, sometimes the best thing to do is run.

The devil is a pretty smart guy, and if you try to defeat him in your own strength, you'll probably fail. He knows your weak points. He knows how to tempt you. When you feel like you're under attack and things are getting crazy in your life, run to Me. I will fight the battle for you.

Sometimes the best offense is a good defense. When you're feeling weak, run into the tower. As you pray to Me and read My Word, I will guard you from the enemy. Run to Me!

Your Strong Tower,
>God

== == ==   == == == == == == == == ==

INVEST IN STRONG FRIENDSHIPS

**As iron sharpens iron,
so one man sharpens another.**

Proverbs   27:17

Dear Child,

>Some friends dull the edge of who you are just by hanging around you. They are time-wasters and procrastinators. Their thoughts are negative, their goals are shallow, and their ideas are weak.

Other friends sharpen you and bring your life into focus. They know what matters and what life is all about. They're not afraid to take a stand on spiritual issues—issues that count. You become a better person just by being around them. Their strength sharpens your character, and as you become stronger, your strengths sharpen theirs.

Invest your time, energy, and friendship in this second kind of friend. You won't regret it.

Your Best Friend,
>God

== == ==   == == == == == == == == ==

BE CREATIVE

Sing to the LORD a new song;
sing to the LORD, all the earth.

| Psalm | 96:1 |

My Child,

>Have you ever seen the exact same sunset twice? It has never happened, and it never will. I've got a million of them. I never run out of new creations. I made you in My image, and I want you to be creative like Me.

Say new prayers. Sing new songs. It's great to have prayers and songs that other people have written. They help when you're stuck or you can't think of anything new to pray or sing. But every now and then, get off by yourself and sing Me a new song. It doesn't matter how it sounds. Just sing what's on your heart. It will sound great to Me, and you'll feel better, too. Be creative. I am.

Your Creator,
>God

== == ==   == == == == == == == == ==

IT AIN'T OVER 'TIL IT'S OVER

**Those who sow in tears
will reap with songs of joy.**

Psalm 126:5

My Child,

>Do you know the story of "The Little Red Hen"? She kept breaking her back to bake this cake. None of her friends would help, but she didn't let that stop her. Finally, the cake was finished, and all her friends wanted a bite. But she said, "No way! I worked on this cake; now it's my time to enjoy it."

My son, Noah, was the same way. I warned him of a coming flood and told him to build a huge boat. So he got busy. Only one problem—up until that time, it had never rained once on earth. Also, Noah was landlocked. There was no water in sight. His friends thought he was an idiot; but when the flood came, they all drowned.

So, if I tell you to do something, just hang in there and do it. Believe Me, you'll be glad you did!

Your Coworker,
>God

== == ==   == == == == == == == == ==

START OFF ON THE RIGHT FOOT

**Satisfy us in the morning with
your unfailing love, that we may sing
for joy and be glad all our days.**

Psalm	90:14

Dear Child of Mine,

>Some people are morning people. They wake up early and energetic, have a mega-breakfast, and get going. Some people are night people. They don't really get moving until noontime, and they do their best thinking late at night.

Which one am I? I'm both, because I never sleep. I'm thinking at night, and I'm up early in the morning. Whether you're a morning or a night person, here's My suggestion for you—right when you get out of bed, take some time to commit your day to Me. If you start your day off with Me, it will surely go better. When you remember that I have everything under control, you'll be much more likely to ask for My help during the day. Try it.

The Inventor of Time,
>God

== == ==   == == == == == == == == ==

THIS BOOK'S FOR YOU!

For the word of God is living and active.
Sharper than any double-edged sword,
it penetrates even to dividing soul
and spirit, joints and marrow; it judges
the thoughts and attitudes of the heart.

Hebrews 4:12

My Child,

>The Bible is not an ordinary book. It's My Word, and My Word is alive with power! Through its pages, I can teach you, help you, comfort you, and make you strong. My Word is a drink of cold water when you're thirsty or a safe place when you're afraid. It's a warm fireside when you're cold or a road map when you're lost.

You can know what is in other books, but My Word is a book that knows what is in you! So read it when you need wisdom or hope. Open its pages every day, and you'll begin to see that My Word is for you, right where you are . . . today.

Your Father and Friend,
>God

== == ==   == == == == == == == == ==

YOU ARE SALT AND LIGHT

You are the salt of the earth. . . .
You are the light of the world.

Matthew | 5:13–14

Dear Child,

>Have you ever tasted food with no seasoning at all? It's blah
and tasteless. That's what people taste when they bite into a
daily diet of life without My love. My love adds the flavor that
makes life spicy and delicious. When you follow Me, you are salt
for a bland and flavorless world.

Have you ever walked into a dark room and groped around
trying to find the light switch? That's how lots of people feel
every day in a world without My light. When you believe in Me,
you become a flashlight, shining My light into the darkness so
people won't stumble and fall.

You bring light by shining My truth into the hype, half-truths, and
outright lies that flourish in this world. Will you be My salt and light?

The Light of the World,
>God

== == ==   == == == == == == == == ==

A SHEPHERD WITH A PLAN

You were lost sheep with no idea who you were or where you were going. Now you're named and kept for good by the Shepherd of your souls.

1 Peter 2:25 | THE MESSAGE

Dear Child,

>Picture a rough, dangerous, uncharted road heading up into craggy hills where wild animals live. Now picture yourself as defenseless as a lamb—no weapon, no map, and no guide—unsure of where you are or where you're going.

Not a comforting picture! But that's a fairly accurate portrait of you before Jesus entered your life. What a different picture He wants to paint of your life if you'll let Him! He knows you, He loves you, and He has a new life for you. He has a road map through those dangerous mountains. He wants to lead you to a place of peace, joy, and happiness with Me.

Jesus is your Shepherd, and He's waiting to lead you. Won't you trust and follow Him?

Your Father,
>God

== == ==   == == == == == == == == ==

I'M WAITING TO BE FOUND

Ask and it will be given to you; seek and you will find; knock and the door will be opened to you. For everyone who asks receives; he who seeks finds; and to him who knocks, the door will be opened.

| Matthew | 7:7-8 |

My Child,

>I've heard you talking about Me with your friends: Is there a God? Isn't there a God? Aren't you getting a little tired of all the talk? Aren't you ready for some truth?

I've got answers for you, if you think you can handle them—not merely intellectual answers, but real, honest-to-God, experience-it-for-yourself answers. Remember when you were a little kid and you used to play hide-and-seek? Maybe you found a great place to hide, but deep inside you were really longing to be found.

Well, I'm like that. I want to be found. So stop all the mental gymnastics, and put your faith in gear. Ask Me. I'll answer. Knock. I'll open the door. Look for Me. I'm waiting to be found.

I Am,
>God

== == ==   == == == == == == == == ==

GO FOR IT!

Don't let anyone look down on you because you are young, but set an example for the believers in speech, in life, in love, in faith and in purity.

1 Timothy · 4:12

My Child,

>You don't have to wait until you're thirty to do big things. Look at all the young people in the Bible who accomplished wonders for Me.

David killed Goliath when all the grown men of Israel wimped out. Young Samuel heard My audible voice while all the adult priests were sleeping. Mary agreed to be the mother of My Son, although she was an unmarried teenage virgin.

I'll work My miracles through anyone who believes My words and obeys My voice. (Believe Me, if I waited around for the perfect, mature Christian, I'd never get anything done!) Regardless of your age, you can do great things through Christ. I believe in you. So go for it!

The One Who Believes in You,
>God

== == ==   == == == == == == == == ==

YOU DON'T VOTE ON GOD

> For the foolishness of God is wiser than
> man's wisdom, and the weakness of God
> is stronger than man's strength.

1 Corinthians   1:25

My Child,

>I'm the smartest Person you will ever know. I'm stronger than the strongest man alive. So I don't have to prove Myself to anyone. Who is smart enough to judge Me? Who is strong enough to fight with Me? Though I tried reasoning with people early in history, they didn't listen. Though I explained Myself perfectly and won every argument, they didn't care.

So instead of arguing, I chose to send My Son to die for you. His love explains Who I am. Jesus on the cross is proof that I exist and that I love you. I hope you can believe that, because it's true. I am Who I am.

The Almighty,
>God

== == ==   == == == == == == == == ==

NOT IN THE COOL CROWD?

As Jesus was walking beside the Sea of Galilee,
he saw two brothers . . . Peter and . . . Andrew.
They were casting a net into the lake,
for they were fishermen. "Come, follow me,"
Jesus said, "and I will make you fishers of men."
At once they left their nets and followed him.

Matthew | 4:18-20

My Child,

>Do you sometimes wish you were part of the "in" crowd—that
you were really cool and were seen as special by your peers?
Jesus and His friends weren't exactly part of the cool group either.

Some people might even have seen them as rejects, but I didn't.
I saw a bunch of ordinary men and women of all ages who
weren't afraid to admit they didn't have it all together. They
wanted more out of life than posing and pretending everything
was alright. They were willing to follow Jesus because they
wanted real life.

Jesus is still looking for the same kind of friends—those who will
share real feelings, bring Him real problems, and let Him know
who they really are so He can be part of their lives. What do you
think? Could you fit in with Jesus' crowd?

His Father and Yours,
>God

== == ==   == == == == == == == == ==

TRY PRAYING INSTEAD

Do not be anxious about anything, but
in everything, by prayer and petition,
with thanksgiving, present your requests
to God. And the peace of God . . . will guard
your hearts and your minds in Christ Jesus.

Philippians 4:6-7

Dear Child,

>What do you worry about? Other people's opinions of you? Your family? Money? Grades? Your safety? Whatever it is, I want to tell you something—worry is a total waste of time. It accomplishes zero.

Instead of spinning your wheels on an endless cycle of worry, try praying instead. Take your worries and shape them into prayers. For instance, say you've been worrying about an argument you had with a friend. Take that worry and pray, "Father, help me repair our friendship. Show me what to do." I will. Then I'll send My peace to replace your worry. Try it! It works!

Your Prayer Partner,
>God

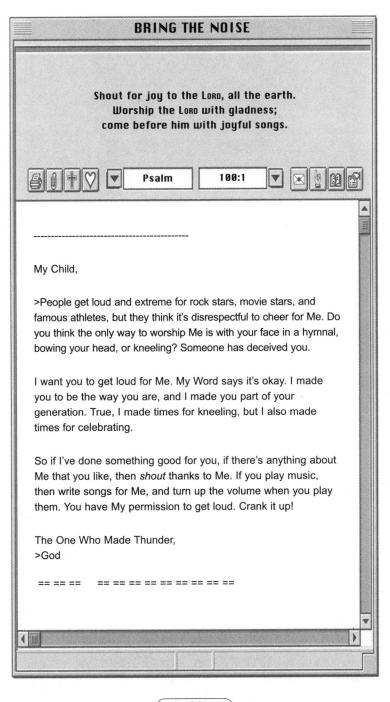

BRING THE NOISE

Shout for joy to the LORD, all the earth.
Worship the LORD with gladness;
come before him with joyful songs.

| Psalm | 100:1 |

My Child,

>People get loud and extreme for rock stars, movie stars, and famous athletes, but they think it's disrespectful to cheer for Me. Do you think the only way to worship Me is with your face in a hymnal, bowing your head, or kneeling? Someone has deceived you.

I want you to get loud for Me. My Word says it's okay. I made you to be the way you are, and I made you part of your generation. True, I made times for kneeling, but I also made times for celebrating.

So if I've done something good for you, if there's anything about Me that you like, then *shout* thanks to Me. If you play music, then write songs for Me, and turn up the volume when you play them. You have My permission to get loud. Crank it up!

The One Who Made Thunder,
>God

== == ==   == == == == == == == == ==

I'VE GOT YOUR BACK

The remnant of Israel . . . will eat and lie down and no one will make them afraid.

| Zephaniah | 3:13 |

Dear Child of Mine,

>In Heaven, nobody's afraid. No one will shoot at you there, because your body will be spiritual, not physical. No one will put you down, because in Heaven, we don't do that. No one will harm you in any way.

On earth, you sometimes need to be on your guard. There are some people you can't trust. But in Heaven, you could take a nap right out in the middle of the street, and no one would even bother you. The reason is, I control what goes on in Heaven, and I keep evil out.

I want to do the same thing here on earth. I want to protect you and guard you. Let Me take the controls of your life now. Trust Me to keep you safe.

Your Bodyguard,
>God

== == ==   == == == == == == == == ==

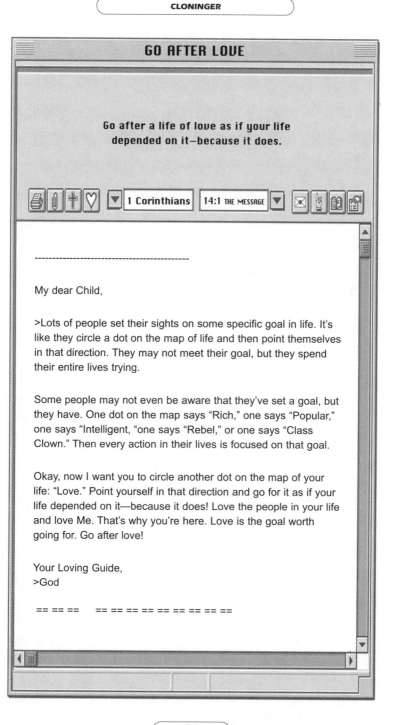

GO AFTER LOVE

**Go after a life of love as if your life
depended on it—because it does.**

1 Corinthians | 14:1 THE MESSAGE

My dear Child,

>Lots of people set their sights on some specific goal in life. It's
like they circle a dot on the map of life and then point themselves
in that direction. They may not meet their goal, but they spend
their entire lives trying.

Some people may not even be aware that they've set a goal, but
they have. One dot on the map says "Rich," one says "Popular,"
one says "Intelligent, "one says "Rebel," or one says "Class
Clown." Then every action in their lives is focused on that goal.

Okay, now I want you to circle another dot on the map of your
life: "Love." Point yourself in that direction and go for it as if your
life depended on it—because it does! Love the people in your life
and love Me. That's why you're here. Love is the goal worth
going for. Go after love!

Your Loving Guide,
>God

== == ==   == == == == == == == == ==

LIGHTS, CAMERA, ACTION

**A thousand may fall at your side,
ten thousand at your right hand,
but it will not come near you.**

Psalm 91:7

My Child,

>Aren't action movies ridiculous? The hero runs through
roadblocks, machine-gun fire, and exploding bombs but never
gets a scratch. Meanwhile, all the hero has to do is look at the
bad guys, and they fall down dead.

Strange as it seems, I want you to think of your life as an action
movie. I'm the Director, and you're the hero. As long as you run
where I (the Director) tell you to, every-
thing will work out fine. Listen to Me, and let Me guide you safely
through the minefields of your life. Then hang onto your popcorn!

Your Director,
>God

== == ==   == == == == == == == == ==

STOP, DROP, AND ROLL?

**When you walk through the fire, you will not be
burned; the flames will not set you ablaze.
For I am the LORD, your God,
the Holy One of Israel, your Savior.**

Isaiah 43:2-3

Dear Child,

>One time, three guys—Shadrach, Meshach, and Abednego—
were thrown into a fiery furnace. The king wanted to burn them
up because they wouldn't bow down and worship him. The fire
was supposed to turn them into toast. But it didn't. In fact, their
clothes didn't even smell like smoke when they walked out! They
were My children, and I protected them.

Now if I can protect three guys thrown into a roaring fire, just
think what I can do for you! Are people making fun of you for
talking about My Son or Me? Is there some area of your life
where you feel vulnerable and unprotected? Are your emotions
burning out of control? Pray and ask Me to deliver you from the
fire. I will do it. Just watch and see.

Your Deliverer,
>God

== == ==   == == == == == == == == ==

I LOVE CRACKPOTS, TOO!

**But we have this treasure in jars of clay
to show that this all-surpassing power
is from God and not from us.**

2 Corinthians **4:7**

My Child,

>Once you believe in Me, I come to live My life in you. One of My favorite things is getting to live in lots of different kinds of people. Then the world sees Me in an amazing variety of human packages: large, small, young, old, tall, short, educated, and uneducated. It's like pouring out a rich, delicious liquid into an assortment of different containers: clay pots, china coffee cups, plastic glasses, crystal pitchers, and pottery mugs. They are all filled with the same stuff—My Spirit—but each one is unique.

Some of My containers even have a few holes and cracks. But I love My crackpots, too! They allow My Spirit to leak out on all the people around them! Let Me fill you up to overflowing.

Your Source and Supply,
>God

== == ==   == == == == == == == == ==

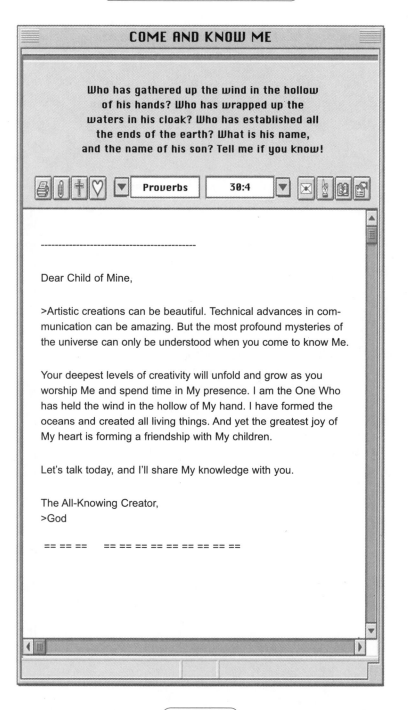

COME AND KNOW ME

Who has gathered up the wind in the hollow of his hands? Who has wrapped up the waters in his cloak? Who has established all the ends of the earth? What is his name, and the name of his son? Tell me if you know!

Proverbs 30:4

Dear Child of Mine,

>Artistic creations can be beautiful. Technical advances in communication can be amazing. But the most profound mysteries of the universe can only be understood when you come to know Me.

Your deepest levels of creativity will unfold and grow as you worship Me and spend time in My presence. I am the One Who has held the wind in the hollow of My hand. I have formed the oceans and created all living things. And yet the greatest joy of My heart is forming a friendship with My children.

Let's talk today, and I'll share My knowledge with you.

The All-Knowing Creator,
>God

== == ==   == == == == == == == == ==

CELEBRATE YOUR UNIQUENESS

Isn't everything you have and everything
you are sheer gifts from God? So what's the
point of all this comparing and competing?

1 Corinthians 4:7 THE MESSAGE

Dear Child of Mine,

>There's no bigger waste of time than comparing yourself to others. Someone will always come out looking better than you look, and that will just make you feel jealous. Or someone else will come out looking worse, and that will make you feel prideful and superior. Believe Me, you don't need those bad attitudes. They will smother your joy like sand on a fire.

Listen, I made you who you are. You're priceless! I gave you wonderful gifts, and only you can fulfill My plan for you. Just as each snowflake is different, so each person is unique and precious to Me. And just as I created thousands of species of fish and flowers in every color of the rainbow, so I created people of all different colors and races. I love variety! Celebrate who you are!

Your Unique Creator,
>God

== == ==   == == == == == == == == ==

I WILL NEVER LET YOU DOWN

The LORD himself goes before you and will be
with you; he will never leave you nor forsake
you. Do not be afraid; do not be discouraged.

| | Deuteronomy | 31:8 | |

Dear Child,

>Nothing hurts more than a good friend who acts like an enemy
or someone you depended on who lets you down.

Jesus understands that feeling. His friends let Him down in major
ways. Judas sold Him out to the Roman authorities for money.
When He was facing the most difficult time of His life—His trial
and crucifixion—He asked His friends to stay awake with Him,
but they all fell asleep. Then after He was arrested He watched
Peter, one of His best friends, lie about their friendship, swearing
three times that he didn't even know Who Jesus was!

When you feel disillusioned about your friends, it helps to
remember they are only human, and human beings sometimes
let you down. But My love is greater. I will never let you down.

Your Friend Forever,
>God

== == ==   == == == == == == == == ==

SLOW DOWN AND LISTEN

Be still, and know that I am God.

| Psalm | 46:10 |

My Child,

>You are always on the move—doing homework, talking on the phone, spending time with your friends—caught up in the hurry and noise of your life.

Do you know that I want to be your friend, too? I have things to say to you—secrets to share. That's why I want you to slow down and listen. Turn off the CD player and the TV for a while. Stop rushing around. When you are quiet, I will speak to your heart. When you are still, you will feel My love.

I am real. I even know what you're thinking about right now, and I'd like to talk to you about it. Until then, I am waiting for you to be still and know Me.

Your Ever-present Friend,
>God

== == ==   == == == == == == == == ==

I KNOW THE WAY

[The man whose delight is in the law of the LORD]
is like a tree planted by streams of water,
which yields its fruit in season and whose leaf
does not wither. Whatever he does prospers.

Psalm	1:3

Dear Child,

>Living for Me is practical. Think about it. If I made the whole
world (which I did), and if I'm perfect and good (which I am), isn't
My way going to be the best way?

My methods aren't meant to burden, frustrate, or limit you. I want
you to be blessed in everything you do. The Bible is My map of
the world. It explains what's out there, and it charts the roads I
want you to take. Disregard the world's directions. They will only
get you lost.

Let Me lead you every day. I know the way.

Your Guide,
>God

== == ==   == == == == == == == == ==

THAT'S MY JOB DESCRIPTION

You are a God of forgiveness, always ready to pardon, gracious and merciful, slow to become angry, and full of love and mercy; you didn't abandon them.

Nehemiah 9:17 TLB

My Child,

>I've noticed that sometimes when you feel like you've blown it, you try to avoid Me. You'd much rather keep your distance, because you don't want to face My anger.

There's something I want you to understand. It doesn't matter how bad you've blown it. Forgiving you is part of My job description. I'm a God of forgiveness—that's Who I am. You're My child. My love and mercy are always within reach. When you make a wrong choice and land in a lot of trouble, I'm standing by just waiting to hear you ask for My help and forgiveness. So ask . . . please. You'll see. I won't abandon you.

Your Forgiver,
>God

== == ==   == == == == == == == == ==

WHAT DOES IT MEAN?

Carrying his own cross, he went out to the place of the Skull (which in Aramaic is called Golgotha). Here they crucified him, and with him two others— one on each side and Jesus in the middle.

John   19:17–18

Dear Child,

>Have you noticed how many people wear a cross as jewelry? You see cross necklaces and cross earrings—gold ones and silver ones, plain ones and fancy ones. In fact, crosses are such common accessories that we rarely stop to think of what they signify.

To the people of Jesus' day, wearing a cross as a decoration would be about like you wearing a little electric chair on a chain around your neck or little electric chairs dangling from your ears! It was not a shiny ornament you could hold in the palm of your hand. It was a rough, heavy instrument of torture that Jesus had to carry on His own back. It was a dreaded device of death to which He was nailed. It cost Him everything.

Now it is a symbol of victory! The cross is empty because Jesus rose from the dead and is seated at My right hand in Heaven. It's a symbol that means everything to Me.

Your Father,
>God

PULL UP A CHAIR AND SIT A WHILE

You prepare a table before me in the presence
of my enemies. You anoint my head
with oil; my cup overflows.

	Psalm	23:5	

My Child,

>Do deadlines, troubles, and chaos plague you right now? Have you ever had to eat and run? Maybe you were late for school, so you had to scarf down your breakfast as you ran out the door.

People who don't trust Me are always on the run—working, striving, trying to outrun whatever it is they fear. But when you place yourself in My hands, you can relax. I'll prompt you to get up a little earlier to spend time with Me, and I will give you peace.

Right in the middle of the world's hurricane of busyness, I'll serve you a sit-down, four-course meal. If you will make time in your day to stop and enjoy our relationship, I'll take care of the things you're worried about. Enjoy Me in the eye of the storm.

Your Peace,
>God

== == ==   == == == == == == == == ==

WHAT LOVE IS

Love is patient . . . kind . . . does not envy . . .
[or] boast . . . is not proud . . . not rude . . .
not self-seeking . . . not easily angered, it keeps
no record of wrongs. Love does not delight in evil
but rejoices with the truth. It always protects,
always trusts, always hopes, always perseveres.

1 Corinthians 13:4-7

My Child,

>Love is more than a casual feeling. It's more than a physical relationship. It's commitment, honor, and caring.

Love is a runner who never gives up on his race, even though he's exhausted. Love is a soldier who gives his coat to his friend even though he himself is freezing. Love is the poor wife who visits her rich neighbor's fancy home and doesn't think, "I wish this were all mine." Love is the football star who wins a trophy but doesn't brag about it to his non-athletic friend. Love is the driver who's been waiting in traffic, but lets another car in line ahead of her. Love is the father who can discipline his child with fairness and no anger. Love is glad when the truth gets told, and it celebrates the good in others.

Love is a song that never ends.

Your Love,
>God

== == ==   == == == == == == == == ==

FIND YOURSELF IN ME

**If your first concern is to look after yourself,
you'll never find yourself. But if you
forget about yourself and look to me,
you'll find both yourself and me.**

Matthew 10:39 | THE MESSAGE

My Child,

>My Kingdom is not always logical, but it is always true. It would seem logical that if you wanted to find yourself you'd go looking for all the things that would make you happy, whether it hurt someone else or not. But My way is exactly opposite.

To find yourself, forget about yourself. Take your mind totally off of you and look to Me instead. Care for others more than yourself.

Let Me lead you along all the surprising trails and across the uncharted oceans of My love. Keep your heart tuned into My channel, and you'll be shocked one day to look up and realize that not only have you found Me, but you have found yourself—the one you were created to be!

Your Road Map,
>God

== == == == == == == == == == == ==

TRUE LOVE

Offer yourselves to God, as those who have been brought from death to life; and offer the parts of your body to him as instruments of righteousness.

| Romans | 6:13 |

My Child,

>I want all of you—body, soul, and spirit—just like a husband wants all of his wife. When you get married, You and your spouse belong to each other. A good marriage is built on sharing every aspect of yourself.

In the same way, if you want to have a relationship with Me, I'm asking you to give Me your whole self. If your mind says, "I love you, God," but you continue using your body in ways that are displeasing to Me, you will never be happy. But if you give your body to Me, I'll bless it and give you physical strength to do the work I've called you to do. I'll use your physical talents, appearance, and athletic ability to help others.

Give Me everything you are, and I will give you all of Me.

Your True Love,
>God

== == ==   == == == == == == == == ==

LET ME COVER YOU

Praise be to the God and Father of our
Lord Jesus Christ, the Father of
compassion and the God of all comfort,
who comforts us in all our troubles.

| | | | | 2 Corinthians | 1:3–4 | | | | |

Dear Child,

>Have you ever slept under a comforter? It's a plush blanket
filled with downy softness that is warm and ultra-cozy. On a cold
night, there's nothing like curling up under a warm comforter.

Think of Me that way. I am your Comforter. Some people think of
Me as a thin sheet or a hard mattress. "I can't go to God," they
say. "He'll just reject me." What a lie! Lies like that are meant to
keep you from running to Me where you belong.

Believe Me, I'm just waiting to hold you and cover you. You can
curl up in My arms and relax from your struggles. I long to hold
you and protect you, My child. I long to comfort you. Run to Me.

Your Father of Compassion,
>God

== == ==   == == == == == == == == ==

I'LL HELP YOU WALK THE PATH

Enter through the narrow gate. The gate is
wide and the road is wide that leads to hell,
and many people enter through that gate.
But the gate is small and the road is narrow that
leads to true life. Only a few people find that road.

Matthew **7: 13-14 NCV**

My Child,

>Every day you're faced with tough decisions and hard choices.
If you're living for Me, it will sometimes feel like you're walking
down a narrow road, trying not to slip off and fall into a ditch.

Sometimes you look around and see most people cruising along
a huge, eight-lane super-highway with lots of room to maneuver.
The big, broad super-highway of life may look easy, but in the
end, its drivers will find it doesn't lead to Me.

How do you stay on the narrow road? Get to know Me. Read My
Word. Let Me lead you and show you the way. Let Me give you
the strength and the balance you need to make the right choices.
You can do it!

The Master Planner,
>God

== == ==   == == == == == == == == ==

I'M ALL YOU NEED

**God my shepherd!
I don't need a thing.**

| 🖨 📎 ✝ 🤍 ▼ | Psalm 23:1 | THE MESSAGE | ▼ | ✉ ✋ 📖 📋 |

Dear Child,

>What if someone offered you anything in the world? What would you ask for? Would it be a fancy new car, a good-looking date, or worldwide fame?

Not many people would say, "No, thanks. I don't really want anything right now. God's guarding Me and caring for me. That's enough." Well maybe you can't imagine yourself ever saying that, but I want you to get a glimpse of how great it would be to know Me that way—to live without anxiety—simply trusting Me to supply all your needs. It's not impossible, you know.

Knowing and trusting in My provision is the key to contented living. And I want to meet more than your physical needs. I want to give you what your heart yearns for—unconditional, unending love. Let Me be enough for you.

Your Shepherd,
>God

== == ==   == == == == == == == == ==

TREASURE YOUR GIFT

It is absolutely clear that God has called
you to a free life. Just make sure that you
don't use this freedom as an excuse to do whatever
you want to do and destroy your freedom. Rather,
use your freedom to serve one another in love.

Galatians 5:13 | THE MESSAGE

Dear Child,

>Suppose you were given a valuable painting and you could do
anything you wanted with it. What would you do? Would you find
the perfect spot for it to hang where it would bring joy and
pleasure to you and all of your guests? Or would you take it
home, smear it with grease, and kick a hole in it?

I'm pretty sure you'd treasure and enjoy it. The life of freedom
My Son is calling you to is also a valuable gift to be treasured
and enjoyed. Find a place of honor for it in your heart, and share
it with friends and strangers alike.

The Gift Giver,
>God

== == ==   == == == == == == == == ==

COME SEE THE LIGHT

Everything was created through him . . .
What came into existence was Life,
and the Life was Light to live by.
The Life-Light blazed out of the darkness;
the darkness couldn't put it out.

John 1:3-5 | **THE MESSAGE**

My Child,

>My Son, Jesus, came into your world as Life itself—powerful, dynamic Life—full of energy and hope. He came into your world as Light, blazing out of the darkness, pushing back the shadows.

All of this Life and Light was contained in a human being, so people didn't understand who they were dealing with when they met Him. He looked like an ordinary person. But He was with Me when the world was made. Every single thing in creation was created through Him. So no wonder people didn't quite "see the Light" when they met Him.

Although they stood in darkness and didn't understand the Light, they could never put it out! He's still shining! Let Him shine in you.

The Father of Light,
>God

== == ==   == == == == == == == == ==

AN ADVENTURE AND A MYSTERY

I have been crucified with Christ. . . . It is no longer
important that I . . . have your good opinion,
and I am no longer driven to impress God.
Christ lives in me. The life you see me living is not
"mine," but it is lived by faith in the Son of God.

Galatians 2:20 THE MESSAGE

My Child,

>This is the most powerful mystery of the faith-life: When you
trust Jesus as your Savior, you crucify your old self. All of the
bad habits, the negative thinking, the low motives, and the gutter
thoughts are put to death.

You don't have to impress anybody with who you are, because
you are *dead!* Then who is walking around in your skin? It's
Jesus in you, making Jesus-choices, thinking Jesus-thoughts,
and bringing His life-giving force into everyday situations! Tell
that old you that he's a dead duck, and you're living as a Christ-
container now. What an adventure!

The Lord in You,
>God

== == ==   == == == == == == == == ==

DON'T STUFF YOUR FEELINGS

**My soul is weary with sorrow;
strengthen me according to your word.**

| Psalm | | 119:28 | |

My Child,

>Have you ever been told, "Big kids don't cry"? I'll never tell you that. It's just not true. I made all of your feelings so that you can respond to life.

What's so mature about stuffing your feelings? What's so admirable about turning off your tears? Life is full of disappointments and sorrows, and if you don't bring them to Me, you'll have to deal with the pain on your own. Stuffed feelings just get worse. They might even resurface later to make you sad when you least expect it.

So bring your sorrow to Me. I will take your sadness and give you My strength. No matter how old you are, you're never too old to cry on My shoulder. Now, tell Me all about it.

Your Loving Father,
>God

== == ==   == == == == == == == == ==

GET INTO THE FIGHT

Fight on for God.

1 Timothy 6:12 TLB

Dear Child,

>Sometimes people give up on life, not because it's too hard, but because it's too easy—not because it's too difficult, but because there's no real challenge worth the risk of fighting.

I want you to be filled with the desire to fight for a higher and greater purpose than yourself. I want you to spend your energy and use your gifts for the greatest good. I want you to know what it's like to stand and fight with Me on the battlefield of faith—to taste the triumph of victory in your life. I don't want you to come to the end of your life and wonder, "Now, what was that all about?" Life is much too valuable. *You* are too valuable.

Hook up with Me, and we'll face our enemies together!

Your Champion,
>God

== == ==   == == == == == == == == ==

GOD IS BIGGER THAN BIG

**The Lord is faithful, and he will strengthen
and protect you from the evil one.**

| | 2 Thessalonians | 3:3 | |

Dear Child,

>Our enemy, the devil, is real, and he wants nothing more than
to ruin your life. If you don't believe it, read the Bible. His
greatest strategy is to make you think he's just a myth. Don't
believe it!

Okay, so what do you do about the devil when you're only five or
six feet tall, and by comparison, the devil is about 1,000 feet
tall? The answer is to trust in Me. If he's that big, then I'm a
million miles tall!

The devil is like a little ant to Me. He's no big deal. You wouldn't
want to take on the neighborhood bully by yourself, but what if you
had your big brother backing you up? Well, I'm your big brother. If
you stick close to Me, I'll help you beat the devil and his crowd.
Pray in the name of Jesus, and watch the enemy tremble.

The All-Powerful One,
>God

== == ==   == == == == == == == == ==

SUNDAY SHOULD BE FUN

**I rejoiced with those who said to me,
"Let us go to the house of the LORD."**

| | Psalm | 122:1 | |

My Child,

>Some people see church as a duty. The thinking goes like this: "Church is boring, but if I go, God will like me better." What a load of junk! I already like you as much as I ever will, so why should your church attendance change My feelings for you?

Church is not supposed to be one of those things you grit your teeth and do because it's good for you, like eating your spinach. It's supposed to make you glad. It's supposed to be a place where you can be real about your relationship with Me—a place where My people meet to encourage each other, pray with each other, and celebrate Me. If that's not what church is like for you, then you're going to the wrong church. Come on, find a place to celebrate Me!

Your Source of Joy,
>God

I AM THE ONE YOU CAN DEPEND ON

Can a mother forget the baby at her breast and
have no compassion on the child she has borne?
Though she may forget, I will not forget you!

Isaiah | **49:15**

My Child,

>What was your life like when you were little? Do you
remember? I do. I was there with you.

Were all your days filled with swings on the playground, presents
under the tree, and homemade cookies in the oven? Or were there
some sad times, disappointments, and loneliness? Were your
parents and siblings always there for you, protecting and helping
you? Were they full of hugs, laughter, and happy surprises? Or
were they sometimes the ones who caused you pain?

Whatever kind of childhood you had (good or bad or in
between), whatever kind of family you grew up in (no one's
home is perfect), you can always depend on My love. I want to
heal your idea of what a parent should be by loving you with the
love of a perfect Parent. Will you let Me start today?

The Father Who's Always Been There,
>God

== == ==   == == == == == == == == ==

SCARS OF REMEMBRANCE

**See, I have engraved you on the palms of
my hands; your walls are ever before me.**

| Isaiah | 49:16 |

Dear Child,

>Did you know My Son, Jesus, has scars of you on the palms of
His hands? He got them by hanging on the cross for you, so that
you could have a relationship with Me. Jesus can't forget you.
Those scars are constant reminders.

Jesus prays for you 24/7 (twenty-four hours a day, seven days a
week). He doesn't sleep and neither do I. Even if you forget
about Me during the day, don't worry; I can't forget about you.
You are never alone or forgotten because Jesus is always
thinking about you. I love you non-stop.

Yours Forever,
>God

== == ==   == == == == == == == == ==

I'M NOT LIKE ANY PERSON YOU KNOW

"For my thoughts are not your thoughts,
neither are your ways my ways," declares the
LORD. "As the heavens are higher than the earth,
so are my ways higher than your ways
and my thoughts than your thoughts."

Isaiah   55:8–9

Dear Child of Mine,

>Some people who know Me say I'm a "trip." I'm not like any person you know, that's for sure.

I'm infinite, which means I always was here and always will be here. That probably blows your mind, because you're not infinite. You have a beginning. Not Me!

I know everything. I know what every single person on earth is thinking and feeling right now, and I can still pay individual attention to each one. And I'm everywhere. There's no place you could go that I wouldn't already be there, even at the bottom of the ocean. I don't have to travel; I'm already there!

If you can't understand what I'm up to right now in your life, that's okay. Trust Me; I know what I'm doing. I have wonderful surprises in store for you.

The Infinite,
>God

== == ==   == == == == == == == == ==

A CHAIN REACTION

**For everything we know about God's Word is
summed up in a single sentence:
Love others as you love yourself.**

Galatians 5:14 THE MESSAGE

Dear Child of Mine,

>When you receive My love, it sets off an amazing chain reaction in your life. First, it mends you where you're broken. It helps you see yourself as I do, and you begin, bit by bit, to make peace with who you are. You recognize your good points, and you stop being so critical of your weaknesses. Next thing you know, you're actually beginning to love yourself a little bit . . . and then a lot.

And as your healthy self-love grows, you discover that you're no longer as critical with yourself. Then gradually, miraculously, you find yourself able to love others in a way you never thought you could, just as you love yourself. This is what happens when you let My love in. It never fails!

The One Who Loves You,
>God

== == ==   == == == == == == == == ==

STOP HITTING YOURSELF

**Many are the woes of the wicked,
but the Lord's unfailing love surrounds
the man who trusts in him.**

| Psalm | 32:10 |

My Child,

>I really don't have to punish people who don't want to do things My way. Sooner or later, they end up punishing themselves. They curse Me, they say they don't need Me, they do what they like, and sure enough, their lives fall apart.

Am I determined to pay them back? Am I cursing them? No, they are punishing themselves by rejecting My goodness in their lives. Living apart from Me is like drinking poison. It's death.

But when you trust Me and do things My way, I surround you, guard you, and help you. Doing things My way is like drinking cold water on a hot day. It's your choice, but if you hide from Me, trouble will surely find you. Please, let Me bless and protect you.

Your Shield,
>God

== == ==   == == == == == == == == ==

LEARN TO LOVE MY RULES

The precepts of the Lᴏʀᴅ are right, giving joy to the heart. The commands of the Lᴏʀᴅ are radiant, giving light to the eyes.

Psalm 19:8

Dear Child,

>Do you get excited about rules? Not many people sit around and say, "Oh, I love the speed limit! It's so wonderful!"

Okay, so why do people get excited about My rules? Because they always lead to a better life. The person on a diet might not like the rules of the diet, but after he loses seventy extra pounds and feels great about his body, he can say, "I love that new diet!" Nobody loves the seatbelt law, until they have a wreck and it saves their life.

My rules are like that. They're not meant to cramp your style. They're meant to set you free and protect you. Rejoice in My boundaries!

Your Guardian,
>God

== == ==   == == == == == == == == ==

THE KEY TO LOVE

If I speak in the tongues of men and of angels,
but have not love, I am only a resounding gong
or a clanging cymbal. . . . if I have a faith that can
move mountains, but have not love, I am nothing.
If I give all I possess to the poor . . .
but have not love, I gain nothing.

1 Corinthians   13: 1-3

My Child,

>I know you want to do great things with your life. I want that for
you, too. But the greatest thing you can do with your life is to
love other people and Me.

No matter what you achieve in life, if you have not loved, your
life will be a failure. You could be a famous rock star or a
powerful politician, but without love, your music would be noise
and your speeches would be empty. You could be a multi-
millionaire with more money than you could ever spend, but
without love, your heart would be bankrupt.

How do you develop that kind of love? Jesus holds the key. Only
He can do it. When you let Him into your life, He will love other
people through you. Then your life will truly count!

Love always,
>God

== == ==   == == == == == == == == ==

I WANT TO FORGIVE YOU

For if you forgive men when they sin against
you, your heavenly Father will also forgive you.
But if you do not forgive men their sins,
your Father will not forgive your sins.

Matthew **6: 14-15**

My Child,

>I want to forgive you, but sometimes I can't because you won't
forgive someone else.

If a group of kids cusses at you, and you hold a grudge about it,
it's just the same as if you walk around all day cussing back at
them. But as soon as you forgive and release them, you are
released to receive My forgiveness. Don't worry about paying
them back. That's My job. But I don't want to pay them back; I
want to forgive them just like I want to forgive you! If you want
Me to have mercy on you, have mercy on other people. If you
want Me to give you a break when you blow it, forgive other
people when they blow it.

When you forgive someone else, watch My love flood into your
life. I've got a dump truck full of love and forgiveness that I want
to pour out on you. Forgive—it's the best thing to do.

Your Dad in Heaven,
>God

== == ==   == == == == == == == == ==

THE CALL TO CARE

So we're not giving up. . . . Even though on
the outside it often looks like things are falling
apart on us, on the inside, where God
is making new life, not a day goes
by without his unfolding grace.

2 Corinthians 4:16 THE MESSAGE

My Child,

>I know that sometimes it's tempting to give up on life.
Sometimes it's hard to find a reason to keep trying.

What makes you feel like throwing in the towel? School?
Grades? Friends? Parents? Money? War? Listen, I want you to
trust Me on this one. Even though the circumstances of life
might look rotten from the outside, when you believe in Me,
there are invisible things going on inside of you. Every day, I'm
unfolding something new and exciting. Your future will be more
amazing than anything you can imagine. Believe Me, it will be
worth hanging on for.

So hang tough. Don't give up! I've got some real surprises for
you.

Your Heavenly Dad,
>God

== == ==   == == == == == == == == ==

THROW OUT THE CATALOG

What kind of deal is it to get everything you want but lose yourself? What could you ever trade your soul for.

Matthew   16:26 THE MESSAGE

Dear Child of Mine,

>Suppose life was like a mail-order catalog, and you could just flip through the pages, selecting everything your heart desired: computers, cars, clothes, fancy vacations, fame, money, power—no limits.

Only the day your order was delivered, it came with a bill that said, "Payment required: Your eternal soul." Would you still place the order? Lots of people do. But they don't fully understand the trade they're making. To begin with, the catalog is a rip-off. It will never deliver in full anyway. And even if it did, no amount of stuff would ever satisfy your soul's restless longing for Me.

So throw out the world's catalog and open up the pages of My plan for you—the Bible. My love delivers what it promises!

Your Loving Dad,
>God

== == ==   == == == == == == == == ==

I BUILT THE CAR

The Lord will fulfill his purpose for me;
your love, O Lord, endures forever—
do not abandon the works of your hands.

Psalm **138:8**

My Child,

>I have a personal interest in your success. You are My creation—a one-of-a-kind original. I've invested creativity, hope, and energy into making you who you are, and I have no intention of quitting on you now.

You're like a finely tuned race car that I've built. On the day of the race, don't you think I'm going to drive that car to victory? I'm not just going to leave it stalled on the side of the road somewhere. I belong in the driver's seat of your life, so put Me there by believing and trusting Me. I know the loops and curves of the track.

I have a plan for your life, child, and I am deeply committed to the results of your race. Don't worry. I haven't abandoned you, and I never will.

Your Driver,
>God

== == ==   == == == == == == == == ==

CHOOSE LIFE!

This day . . . I have set before you life
and death, blessings and curses.
Now choose life, so that you . . . may live.

| | | | | ▼ | Deuteronomy | 30:19 | ▼ | | | |

Dear Child of Mine,

>I want you to choose life. Choosing life means looking at life
with hope and love rather than with fear and doubt.

Choosing life means caring about others instead of obsessing
about yourself. Choosing life means watching a sunset or
encouraging a friend, instead of vegging out in front of the TV set
every night. Choosing life means trusting Me to help you do the
hard things, instead of giving up before you even try. Choosing
life is laughing with children instead of doubting with skeptics.
Choosing life is celebrating your own gifts instead of being
envious of someone else's.

Choosing life means standing for what's right and true, even if someone thinks you're a geek for doing it. Choosing life is loving Me.

Yours for Life,
>God

== == ==   == == == == == == == == ==

LET ME BE YOUR TREE HOUSE

**You are my hiding place; you will protect
me from trouble and surround
me with songs of deliverance.**

| Psalm | 32:7 |

My Child,

>Is there a special place you go to get away from everything and
everybody? Some people like to climb a tree. Others hide away
in a corner of their backyard. Concealing yourself in a physical
place helps when people and circumstances are just too much
for you.

But where can you hide from your emotions and fears? Let Me
be your hiding place. When things get rough, run to Me when
you need shelter from your life. Pray and read My words in the
Bible. Then listen. Not only will I shelter you, I will surround you
with encouraging songs. I will sing you back to peace. Come
away with Me to our secret place. I'll meet you there.

Your Shelter,
>God

== == ==   == == == == == == == == ==

WHAT TO WEAR EVERY DAY

Clothe yourselves with compassion, kindness, humility, gentleness, and patience.

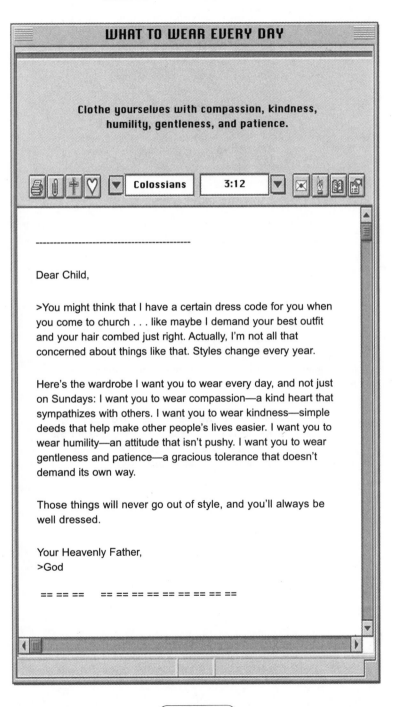

Colossians 3:12

Dear Child,

>You might think that I have a certain dress code for you when you come to church . . . like maybe I demand your best outfit and your hair combed just right. Actually, I'm not all that concerned about things like that. Styles change every year.

Here's the wardrobe I want you to wear every day, and not just on Sundays: I want you to wear compassion—a kind heart that sympathizes with others. I want you to wear kindness—simple deeds that help make other people's lives easier. I want you to wear humility—an attitude that isn't pushy. I want you to wear gentleness and patience—a gracious tolerance that doesn't demand its own way.

Those things will never go out of style, and you'll always be well dressed.

Your Heavenly Father,
>God

== == ==   == == == == == == == == ==

I AM WITH YOU

The LORD is close to the brokenhearted and saves those who are crushed in spirit.

| | Psalm | 34:18 | |

Dear Child,

>My Son Jesus hung out with brokenhearted people—two sisters who had just lost their brother, a man whose young son had died, another man who'd been blind his whole life, a little shrimp of a tax collector who was hated by everybody . . . the list goes on and on. He was close to the people who needed Him, and so am I.

Sadness is not new to Me. I have experienced the death of My Son. I know what it's like to be sad. So if you're sad, you are not alone. If you feel like you just can't go on, turn to Me. I am here to dry your tears and ease your pain. I care for you.

Your Lord,
>God

== == ==   == == == == == == == == ==

GET CAUGHT DOING IT RIGHT

**Whatever you do, work at it with all your heart,
as working for the Lord, not for men. . . .
It is the Lord Christ you are serving.**

Colossians   3:23-24

My Child,

>When no one is looking, it's tempting to cheat. Maybe you wouldn't even call it cheating. Maybe you'd just call it slacking, or easing off.

But to make a habit of slacking is to lose the joy in your work. Doing a job right makes you feel good, because I made you to enjoy hard work—to enjoy doing your best.

So don't work hard because you think I'm standing over you cracking the whip. I'm not. Don't even work hard to please other people. Do your best whether people are watching you or not. Then when your boss or teacher does pop in unexpectedly, they'll wonder why you're working so hard. But we'll know why. It'll be our secret!

Your Heavenly Employer,
>God

== == ==   == == == == == == == == ==

MY OFFER STILL STANDS

Yes, and from ancient days I am he.
No one can deliver out of my hand.
When I act, who can reverse it?"

Isaiah 43:13

Dear Child,

>Don't you hate it when people promise something good, and
then they change their minds? "Oh, I would have bought that for
you, but they raised the price." "I know I said I'd be there, but
something important came up." I'm not like that. If I say I'll be
there, I'll be there.

When I do something, no one can undo it. I have chosen you to
be part of My family, and that offer is always open. I will never
withdraw it. I want to spend as much time with you as I can. I am
never too busy for you—ever! I love you, and I always want to
be with you. That will never change.

Your Promise-Keeper,
>God

== == ==   == == == == == == == == ==

I'LL MEET YOU IN YOUR ROOM

In my Father's house are many rooms; if it
were not so, I would have told you.
I am going there to prepare a place for you.
And if I go and prepare a place for you,
I will come back and take you to be
with me that you also may be where I am.

John   14:2-3

Dear Child of Mine,

>My Son, Jesus, can't lie. So when He says there's a home in
Heaven for those who follow Him, it's true.

Heaven is real—as real as anything you can touch right now. It's
actually *more* real, because it will last forever, and the stuff you
can touch now will eventually turn to dust.

So what's up here? Well, I have a room all ready for you. All the
things you love are in it, and some things are there that you will
love and don't even know about yet. Ever heard of sky-blading?
Never mind. You'll see.

The best news is, I'm here waiting for you. When you're finally
home with Me, it will be awesome forever. I'm looking forward to
seeing you face to face, but first, you've got a lot of living to do
on earth. So hang in there!

Your Heavenly Father,
>God

== == ==   == == == == == == == == ==

GET REAL

Are you tired? Worn out? Burned out on religion? Come to me. Get away with me and you'll recover your life. I'll show you how to take a real rest.

| Matthew | 11:28 THE MESSAGE |

My Child,

>There is nothing more exhausting than "playing church," acting like you've got it all together while inside you're aching, lonely, and needing to be real with someone. That kind of religious "play acting" is the road to spiritual burnout.

Besides, it's not how things work with Me. Never has been. If there's one place on earth you can be real, it's with Me. If there's one place you can give the act a rest, it's in My presence. I'm not interested in anyone's performance. I want to make contact with the real you. I want to heal what's hurting in you, to forgive what needs forgiving, to refresh you totally. Come away with Me and let Me fill you with new life. Give it a rest.

Your Heavenly Dad,
>God

== == ==   == == == == == == == == ==

I ANSWER PRAYER

Jesus answered . . . "Whatever you ask for in prayer, believe that you have received it, and it will be yours."

| | Mark | 11:22,24 | |

Dear Child,

>Will I give you everything you ask for? Well, answering prayers is My business. Some people say, "Be careful what you pray for, because it just *might* happen." I say, *"if* you pray according to what I want, it *will* happen."

Now don't come to Me with a prayer about wanting the universe to fit into your baseball glove or wanting to own all the cars in America. Get real. But if there's something you want to ask Me—something you just can't get out of your head—then that prayer is probably from Me. Pray it back to Me and believe that I'll answer it.

Remember, I can do anything. No one has ever trusted Me too much. Just ask Me.

The Giver,
>God

== == ==   == == == == == == == == ==

SAY THE WELCOMING WORD

It's the word of faith that welcomes God to go
to work and set things right for us. . . . Say the
welcoming word to God—"Jesus is my Master"—
embracing, body and soul. . . . You're not "doing"
anything; you're simply calling out to God,
trusting him to do it for you. That's salvation.

Romans 10:9 | THE MESSAGE

My Child,

>Some people have a totally wrong idea of what it is to have a
relationship with Me. They come at Me with all sorts of
accomplishments, trying to impress Me with what good people
they are. (If they're so good, what do they need Me for?)

Don't they realize I'm already aware of their mistakes?
Approaching Me with a false pride is not the way to impress Me.
I want to be friends with the person who'll go out on a limb and
express faith in Me and My Son . . . the person who'll welcome
our work . . . the person who's not too proud to show need.

You don't need to wear a religious mask or put on a big charade.
When you tell Jesus you believe in Him and need Him, you can
walk right in My front door. It's that simple.

Lord of All,
>God

== == ==   == == == == == == == == ==

WHAT WILL HAPPEN WHEN THE STORM COMES

Unless the Lord builds the house,
its builders labor in vain.

Psalm 127:1

Dear Child,

>In some parts of the world, where storms are terrible and regular, people build their houses out of bamboo and paper. Every year or so, storms wipe out everything. Because the people realize their houses are just going to get knocked down, they don't waste their time and effort trying to build strong houses. This is smart.

You can't build a strong, successful life all on your own. Apart from Me, you'll work to make your life look good, but something will always come along to knock it down. I am the only One with enough power and wisdom to build a life that will withstand the storms.

So get smart. Forget your own plans. Let Me show you My plans and help you build a strong, successful life. My work lasts.

The Master Architect,
>God

== == ==   == == == == == == == == ==

CAN I HELP?

**Commit to the LORD whatever you do,
and your plans will succeed.**

Dear Child,

>I want to be involved in your life—not just your prayer life or your church life—but your *whole* life. Even if you're just training your dog, or writing a story, or decorating your room, every activity goes better with Me.

If what you're doing is not wrong, then bring it to Me and ask for My help. Think about it: I painted every sunset and created all the flowers, so I'm pretty handy at helping to decorate a room. When you commit a project to Me, I'll work with you to make it better. I'm not as interested in the project as I am in our relationship. I love doing things with you. I want to be a part of your whole life. Please share your plans with Me.

Your Creator,
>God

== == ==   == == == == == == == == ==

I STILL SHOW UP IN PERSON

Jesus answered: . . . "Anyone who has seen me has seen the Father."

| John | 14:9 |

My Dear Child,

>Why don't I show up in person and let everybody see how real I am? I did! Instead of just looking down from Heaven, I came to earth myself in the life of My Son, Jesus.

Jesus was born to simple parents and lived in a small village. He went to school and learned a trade. Then he spent three years telling people about Me. For that, He was arrested, tried, found guilty, beaten, spit on, and nailed to a cross where He suffered and died. Some friends buried Him in a borrowed tomb, but by the power of My Holy Spirit, I brought Him back to life to live forever!

In Jesus, I showed up in person. And I'm still showing up in the lives of those who trust Me and let Me work in their lives.

Personally,
>God

== == ==   == == == == == == == == ==

MAKE A ROAD IN YOUR HEART

> Prepare a road for the Lord to travel on!
> Widen the pathway before him! Level the mountains!
> Fill up the valleys! Straighten the curves!
> Smooth out the ruts! And then mankind
> shall see the Savior sent from God.

Luke   3:4-6 TLB

My Child,

>I want you to make a road in your heart which Jesus can travel on. With the help of My Holy Spirit, cut down all the undergrowth of meaningless activities. Level the mountains of self-centeredness and conceit. Fill up the valleys of low self-worth and depression. Straighten out any crooked motives or twisted justifications. Smooth out the ruts of procrastination and laziness.

With a smooth road to travel on, Jesus can move freely through your life, making the kind of difference He longs to make in you. He can lead and guide you, and you will find a new freedom to follow Him. And the more you follow Him, the more you will be like Him. Then the people around you will be able to see Him in you!

Your Way-Maker,
>God

== == ==   == == == == == == == == ==

THE LAMB THAT WAS A LION

**He was led like a lamb to the slaughter,
and as a sheep before her shearers is silent,
so he did not open his mouth.**

Isaiah	53:7

Dear Child,

>Jesus lived a perfect life as a human being. Before He left
Heaven, I gave Him a job to do on earth, and He did it exactly
like I told Him.

After He was tortured and handed over to be crucified, Jesus had
a chance to defend Himself. After all, He was perfectly innocent.
And He was so powerful, He could have destroyed all of His
accusers by just waving His hand . . . but He didn't. Jesus obeyed
Me and kept His mouth shut so that He would die on the cross,
taking all your mistakes and wrongdoing with Him. His sacrificial
death earned you the chance to know My forgiveness . . . and Me.

So understand, the strongest person isn't the one who blows up
everything or yells the loudest about how unfair life is. The
strongest person is the one who silently obeys Me, even in the
face of false accusations. Be strong by being humble.

The Father of Jesus,
>God

== == ==   == == == == == == == == ==

GET SET FREE

**Then you will know the truth,
and the truth will set you free.**

| John | 8:32 |

My Child,

>Truth is the most freeing thing in the world. When you know the truth and live your life by it, you don't have to make up any excuses or alibis.

When you live in a truthful way, you aren't saying something to one person and something else to another person and then trying to remember what you said to whom. You can speak your mind and show your feelings without fear. You can simply be yourself and know it's enough.

I want you to know the truth deep inside yourself, so that you don't have to waste your energy untangling a lot of lies, fibs, and half-truths. I want you to experience the freedom that comes with being totally honest. Most of all, I want you to know Jesus. He is the Truth.

Your Father,
>God

== == ==   == == == == == == == == ==

IT'S THE TRUTH

Every word of God is flawless; he is a shield
to those who take refuge in him.
Do not add to his words, or he will
rebuke you and prove you a liar.

Proverbs 30:5-6

Dear Child,

>If I said it in My Book, the Bible, then you can believe it's true. I can't lie. You can put all your faith in Me. The problem is, people just don't believe Me enough.

Will you trust Me? Then pray to Me. Trust Me by doing things My way, even when it doesn't seem to make sense. Some doubters say My Book is full of fairy tales. They try to explain away My miracles as if they didn't happen. But they *did* happen.

Put Me to the test yourself. I protect people who rely on Me. The best way to find out if I'm really "the net under your trapeze" is to let go and go for it. If you fall, I'll catch you. Really! Every promise in the Bible is true. Try Me and see.

Your Trustworthy Friend,
>God

== == ==   == == == == == == == == ==

IT'S OKAY TO HAVE DOUBTS

Then he said to Thomas, "Put your finger here; see my hands. Reach out your hand and put it into my side. Stop doubting and believe." Thomas said to Him, "My Lord and my God!"

| John | 20:27-28 |

My Child,

>Jesus is not surprised by your doubts. Even His disciples doubted Him sometimes. After His crucifixion, Jesus shocked them all by showing up in person. To prove Who He was, He let them touch the wounds in His hands where the nails had been driven, and the wound in His side where He had been stabbed. They were convinced.

They couldn't wait to tell Thomas, who hadn't been with them when Jesus appeared. But Thomas said, "Sorry, I'm not taking your word for it. I've got to see this for myself." One week later, Jesus showed up again, and the first thing He said was, "Come on over here, Thomas. See for yourself. Touch My wounds." That's all it took. Thomas believed.

So don't feel bad when you have doubts. Jesus wants to help you believe in Him. So do I.

Your Father,
>God

== == ==   == == == == == == == == ==

TRUST ME IN THE HARD TIMES

Though he slay me, yet will I hope in him.

Job   13:15

My Child,

>Job was a man who lived more than three thousand years ago.
He had a pretty horrible life for a while. All of his children died on
the same day. Then he got a horrible skin disease that was so
bad, he scratched his sores with broken pottery just to get some
relief. And he lost everything he owned.

All Job's friends told him to just curse Me and die. But Job said,
"Even if God kills me, I will still trust Him." Job knew that I was
good. He also knew that he had done nothing wrong. Job didn't
know why he was suffering, and he questioned Me. But Job
never gave up on Me.

If you have unanswered questions, that's all right. Someday you
will understand everything. But for now please believe that I love
you, and don't give up on Me. Trust Me in the hard times.

Your Faithful Friend,
>God

== == ==   == == == == == == == == ==

WATCH HOW I DO IT

> Walk with me and work with me—watch
> how I do it. Learn the unforced rhythms of
> grace. I won't lay anything heavy or
> ill-fitting on you. Keep company with me
> and you'll learn to live freely and lightly.

| Matthew 11:29-30 | THE MESSAGE |

My Child,

>Some people will do everything they can to complicate the life
of faith. They'll try to strangle you with rules and trip you up with
regulations. And they'll appoint themselves as watch dogs of
your faith if you let them.

Steer clear of those people! If you don't, they'll strip the beauty
and freedom out of your heart as quickly as I pour it in. The best
way to learn to travel the faith journey is to walk with Me. The
surest way to figure out how it works is to work with Me.

There is a freedom that you'll learn to put on every day—a
freedom tailor-made for you. There's a dance of grace so joyful it
makes you feel like you're flying. Watch and follow Me.

Love always,
>God

== == ==   == == == == == == == == ==

LIVE YOUR LIFE

We can say without any doubt or fear,
"The Lord is my Helper and I am not afraid
of anything that mere man can do to me."

Hebrews	13:6 TLB

My Child,

>Don't lock your heart away in a safe little room because you're afraid of being hurt. It will become a jail cell for you. And a heart that's locked in jail will never learn to live.

I want you to unlock your emotions. Take on a challenge. Move out into the flow of life and invest your feelings in other people. Sure, it may be risky. I'm not saying that everything you try will be painless or work out perfectly. You will get hurt from time to time. Your heart may get broken.

But whatever happens, I will be with you to heal your hurts and put your broken heart back together. Don't bury your life . . . live it!

The Lord of Life,
>God

== == ==   == == == == == == == == ==

I GIVE THE HOLY SPIRIT

And if the Spirit of him who raised Jesus from the dead is living in you, he who raised Christ from the dead will also give life to your mortal bodies through his Spirit, who lives in you.

| Romans | 8:11 |

My Child,

>What if the spirit of Michael Jordan possessed you and suddenly you could play basketball just like him? You probably wouldn't be as tall as he is, but I imagine your game would improve considerably. Your friends would say, "Man, where did you learn to do *that!*"

Becoming a Christian means that you are possessed by My Spirit—the Holy Spirit. It may sound scary, but it's really a great thing. My Spirit comes to live inside of you. My Spirit possessed Jesus and raised Him from the dead. So if My Holy Spirit is that powerful and that good, don't you want Him living in you? My Spirit in you will do things *through you* that you could never do alone.

Ask My Spirit into your life. I want to empower you.

Your One and Only Lord,
>God

== == ==   == == == == == == == == ==

DEPEND ON ME

**Jesus Christ is the same yesterday
and today and forever.**

| Hebrews | 13:8 |

My Child,

>A lot of kids you know probably run their lives based on their
feelings. Maybe they've been taught to believe that being true to
their feelings means they are being true to themselves. But think
about it. Feelings are the most unpredictable, undependable
things in the world.

If the gauges in your car registered your feelings, one minute
your engine would be running hot, and the next minute, cold.
One minute the gauge would show a full tank of gas, and the
next minute you would be on empty.

But My character, My strength, and My love are unchangeable. I
love you today and that is never going to change. It's so much
better to run your life based on the steady, unchangeable gauges
of Who I am and how much I love you. Depend on Me.

Your Father,
>God

== == ==   == == == == == == == == ==

I'M TALKING TO YOU

**Listen and hear my voice;
pay attention and hear what I say.**

| Isaiah | 28:23 |

My Child,

>There is so much noise all around you: traffic, television, loud music in passing cars, babies crying, and people talking, shouting, or laughing. It's hard to hear your own thoughts much less listen for My quiet voice.

But I'm asking you to listen. I want to get a word in edgewise. I have personal words for your life—words of love, encouragement, and guidance. One of the best ways to hear from Me is by reading the Bible. Yes, the Bible. It's the bestseller that tops all bestseller lists. Begin in Mark or John. Before you read, ask My Holy Spirit to bring the words to life for you. Plug in your heart when you read, and you will hear Me. After you read, talk to Me. Ask Me anything you like. Then listen for My answer.

Your Friend,
>God

== == ==   == == == == == == == == ==

THINGS LOOK GREAT FROM UP HERE

It is God who arms me with strength and makes
my way perfect. He makes my feet like the feet
of a deer; he enables me to stand on the heights.

Psalm **18:32-33**

Dear Child,

>If you could be either a submarine captain or an airplane pilot,
which would you be? Most people say they would want to be a
pilot, but why? Well, the view certainly is better. In a plane, you
get a sense of perspective. You are above the action, not under it.

Do you ever feel like you're drowning in the events of your own
life? When you get that underwater feeling, I want to lift you up
and give you My birds-eye view of your life. I can see into the
future, and I know how everything's going to work out.

Talk to Me. Ask Me questions, and then find My answers in the
Bible. Once you begin to see that I'm in control, you'll feel lifted
up. Let Me change your point of view.

Your Strength-Giver,
>God

== == ==   == == == == == == == == ==

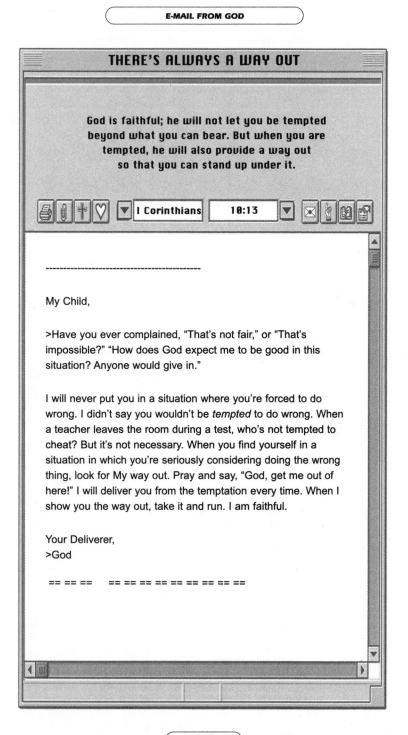

THERE'S ALWAYS A WAY OUT

God is faithful; he will not let you be tempted
beyond what you can bear. But when you are
tempted, he will also provide a way out
so that you can stand up under it.

I Corinthians | **10:13**

My Child,

>Have you ever complained, "That's not fair," or "That's
impossible?" "How does God expect me to be good in this
situation? Anyone would give in."

I will never put you in a situation where you're forced to do
wrong. I didn't say you wouldn't be *tempted* to do wrong. When
a teacher leaves the room during a test, who's not tempted to
cheat? But it's not necessary. When you find yourself in a
situation in which you're seriously considering doing the wrong
thing, look for My way out. Pray and say, "God, get me out of
here!" I will deliver you from the temptation every time. When I
show you the way out, take it and run. I am faithful.

Your Deliverer,
>God

== == ==   == == == == == == == == ==

I GIVE NEW HOPE

**[The Lord] has sent me
to bind up the brokenhearted.**

Isaiah 61:1

Dear Child,

>Have you ever seen a dog after his master dies? Sometimes the dog will mope around the house and howl for days. His entire purpose in life is gone. That dog is brokenhearted.

A brokenhearted person has hoped and been betrayed. Can anyone mend a heart that's been broken? My Son can do it. He knows all about your hopes and dreams. He knows how you've been hurt, and He knows how to give you hope again. If you will trust Jesus to heal your hurt, He will come in and give you a new heart. All you have to do is ask.

Your Heart-Mender,
>God

== == ==   == == == == == == == == ==

LET YOUR ACTIONS DO THE TALKING

**Dear children, let us not love with words
or tongue but with actions and in truth.**

| | | | | | 1 John | | 3:18 | | | | | |

Dear Child,

>Here's a little "pop quiz." Suppose a girl was dying of thirst by
the side of the road and two of her friends came along.

The first one looked down at the thirsty girl and said, "Oh, I hate
to see you suffering like this. I'd love to help you out, but I'm late
for a hair appointment. Sorry." But the second girl ran home, got
a thermos of cold water, and ran back. She held the water to the
thirsty girl's lips and helped her drink. Now the question. Which
of the two girls was a true friend? The one who talked a good
game, or the one who brought the water?

So what's My point? Keep words to a minimum and let your
actions do the talking.

Your Father and Friend,
>God

== == ==   == == == == == == == == ==

HAVE A LITTLE FAITH

We live by faith, not by sight.

2 Corinthians | 5:7

My Child,

>You may think you're a person who lacks faith, but you have more faith than you think you do. You use it every day in a million little ways.

For instance, do you test the strength of a chair to see if it will hold you before sitting down? No, you have faith that it will hold your weight. Do you run a lab test on your food before eating it to make sure it isn't poisoned? No, you have faith that the food is safe, so you chow down.

If you needed visual, scientific proof of everything before you acted on it, you'd turn into a paranoid freak who couldn't make a decision. But you don't. You live by faith in lots of other things. How about putting a little faith in Me where it can do some good!

The Invisible,
>God

== == ==   == == == == == == == == ==

DON'T COUNT SHEEP, PRAY!

On my bed I remember you; I think of you through the watches of the night.

Psalm 63:6

My Dear Child,

>If you can't sleep at night, pray. If the devil is keeping you awake, just pray. He'll get off your case; I guarantee it.

Sometimes I'll wake you up at night. Don't wonder about it—just pray your way back to sleep. Sometimes someone on the other side of the world needs prayer, and I will wake you up to pray for them. If you wake up late at night, ask Me, "Lord, what is it?" I will tell you how to pray, and then you pray that way. It doesn't have to make sense why or who.

Remember, I never sleep. So don't be surprised if you wake up in the night and find Me there. Make Me part of your nighttime, too.

Your Lord,
>God

== == ==   == == == == == == == == ==

I WILL LIFT YOU UP

**Humble yourselves before the Lord,
and he will lift you up.**

James 4:10

My Child,

>Look around you. Who are the people that are the most
stressed out and unhappy? Aren't they the ones who are
constantly trying to beat other people out? The ones who put
other people down to make themselves look good?

Let Me tell you a secret. You can be a winner without putting
anybody down. You can pull for others instead of trying to beat
them out. Your only competition should be between yourself as
you are and yourself as you want to be. In that competition, your
own progress will be your prize.

As you learn to always pull for others without pushing yourself to
the front, you'll find that I'll lift you up.

Your Father,
>God

== == ==   == == == == == == == == ==

BEING A CHRISTIAN IS SIMPLE, NOT EASY

**These are written that you may believe
that Jesus is the Christ, the Son of God, and
that by believing you may have life in his name.**

| John | 20:31 |

My Child,

>Becoming a Christian is not hard. In fact it is so simple any child can do it. If you believe that Jesus is My Son Who came to forgive people and you want to be forgiven, then you can be a Christian.

Although becoming a Christian is simple, living like one can be difficult at times. Standing up for what's right when everyone else is doing what's wrong is hard. Caring about people who don't treat you with any respect is hard. Being My person in places where people don't believe in Me or honor My words is hard.

But the good news is that when you make the simple decision to follow My Son, I am there to help you through the hard times.

Your Redeemer,
>God

TRUST ME

Let us hold unswervingly to the hope we profess, for he who promised is faithful.

| | Hebrews | 10:23 | |

My Child,

>There's a saying, "Who can you trust these days?" Maybe you don't trust your parents, your friends, or even the leaders at your church. Maybe you have a good reason to distrust them.

However, the question is, do you trust Me? If anyone ever hurt you, that was not I. I will never hurt you. In fact I hate it when you're hurt. Know that I exist, that I'm powerful enough to save you, and that I love you intensely. People may let you down, but I never will.

Don't stop trusting Me just because some Christians do cruel or stupid things. I am faithful. My words in the Bible are true. Don't give up on Me, because I will never give up on you.

Your Faithful Father,
>God

== == ==   == == == == == == == == ==

WANT MY OPINION?

He has showed you, O man, what is good.
And what does the LORD require of you?
To act justly and to love mercy and
to walk humbly with your God.

Micah **6:8**

Dear Child,

>What's important to you? Some people think money is the name of the game. They keep up with the latest investment schemes so they can score big bucks. Some people think outward appearances are where it's at. They invest everything in trying to look good.

Are you interested in My opinion? Three things really matter to Me: First, I want you to act justly. When you make a promise, keep it. Stand by your beliefs. Second, I want you to love mercy. That means you can't hold grudges. You have to be willing to forgive. And third, I want you to live humbly with Me—not always wanting your own way—but learning to want mine. It means knowing you are My child.

Your Father,
>God

== == ==   == == == == == == == == ==

I KNOW YOU BETTER THAN YOU KNOW YOURSELF

All a man's ways seem right to him, but the LORD weighs the heart.

| Proverbs | 21:2 |

Dear Child,

>Do you realize that you can think you're right and still be totally wrong? Have you ever argued, "The movie starts at seven-fifteen, I'm sure of it!" And then you show up, and the movie has been on since six o'clock? Or maybe you've convinced yourself that you're being nice to someone for the right reasons, but really you're just being nice to them to copy their homework.

Whatever it is, you may fool yourself and others, but you can't fool Me. I can see right through to the core of your heart. I know when you're being honest, and when you're just lying to yourself. If you really want to know right from wrong, don't trust yourself. Trust Me. Trust My Bible. I'll never lie to you.

Your Conscience,
>God

== == ==   == == == == == == == == ==

DON'T WASTE TIME

**Teach us to number our days aright,
that we may gain a heart of wisdom.**

| Psalm | 90:12 |

Dear Child,

>"Time is of the essence." I'm sure you've heard that expression before. It just means that time matters.

Do you realize that this is the only today you'll ever have? You can't live in yesterday, and you can't live in tomorrow. You can only live now. With that in mind, don't waste your time. You only have so much of it. It may seem like you will live forever on earth, but you won't. So why waste time on destructive feelings like anger and bitterness? Learn to forgive.

Don't waste time doing unimportant things. Sure, have fun . . . relax. But don't just sit around. I have wonderful things for you to accomplish and experience, and you won't discover them by sitting in front of the television all day. I have something better for you.

The Creator of Time,
>God

== == ==   == == == == == == == == ==

JESUS DIDN'T LIVE IN A PALACE

I will put my dwelling place among you, and
I will not abhor you. I will walk among you
and be your God, and you will be my people.

Leviticus **26:11,12**

My Child,

>One time in France, the workers were rioting because they had
no more bread to eat. The clueless queen heard about it and
said, "Well, just let them eat cake." She was so used to being
surrounded by wealth and luxury that she couldn't even imagine
people with no food at all.

Some people think I'm like that queen. "God lives in Heaven.
How can He know what we humans are going through?" But I do
know, because I chose to live with you. So much so, that My
Son, Who is God, too, became a man. He didn't just visit earth,
He became a human. On the cross, Jesus felt all the hurt any
man can ever feel. So yes, I feel your pain. I know what it's like.
I am with you.

Your Father,
>God

== == ==   == == == == == == == == ==

YOU ARE FREE!

Christ has set us free to live a free life.
So take your stand! Never again let anyone
put a harness of slavery on you.

Galatians 5:1 | **THE MESSAGE**

My Child,

>Jesus paid with His blood to give you spiritual freedom. He blazed a trail from chains to liberty. He paid the ultimate price to cut you loose from the "shoulds" and "oughts" of the religious police.

Here's how to *live* free: Know that I am real. You don't have to hope I'm real or pretend I'm real. I am real!

Get to know Me. How? Prayer is a great way. So is Bible reading. But don't make those things into hard-and-fast rules. I won't love you one bit more because you pray or read the Bible a certain amount of time each day. But they will help you to know Me better. That will be the payoff.

Love everyone—even those who don't understand the free life. And finally, don't let anyone put you into a spiritual straight jacket. You are free!

Your Emancipator,
>God

== == ==   == == == == == == == == ==

JUST COME TO ME

I do not concern myself with great matters or things too wonderful for me. But I have stilled and quieted my soul; like a weaned child with its mother.

Psalm 131:1-2

Dear Child of Mine,

>Some people are curious. They want to understand how everything works, and that's good. But no one will ever fully understand Me. You'll go crazy trying to prove to someone that I really exist!

You don't need to know everything about Me in order to trust Me though. Think about a light switch. I bet you don't fully understand how a light switch triggers electrons to run down a wire and power a lightbulb. Even electricians and physicists are amazed at how this works. But that doesn't keep you from turning on the lights.

Trust Me. I work for you. I am real. So come to Me as a little child and let Me meet your needs. You don't need to prove My existence to be My friend.

Just Know that I Am,
>God

== == ==   == == == == == == == == ==

LEARN TO BE A LOVE RECEIVER

I tried keeping rules and working my head off to
please God, and it didn't work. So I quit being
a "law man" so that I could be God's man.

Galatians 2:19 | THE MESSAGE

Dear Child,

>Unless you can obey every law down to the last letter, you
can't say that you've kept the law. And no one can keep every
letter of every law. So no one can make it as a law keeper. You
can't get in good with Me by working hard enough either.

So if you can't earn your way into My heart by being good
enough or working hard enough, what can you do? You can only
be mine by accepting and embracing My love. I've made it so
simple that it actually makes some people mad. They'd rather do
something for Me than receive what I've done for them. They'd
rather give Me something than receive the gift I have for them.

The truth remains—you can only be God's man or woman when
you learn to be a love receiver.

Your Father,
>God

== == ==   == == == == == == == == ==

I BRING THE JOY

The Sovereign Lord . . . has sent me to . . . provide
for those who grieve in Zion—to bestow on them
a crown of beauty instead of ashes, the oil of
gladness instead of mourning, and a garment
of praise instead of a spirit of despair.

Isaiah | 61:1–3

My Child,

>You know you're sad when you're at Disney World in the middle
of all the color and excitement, and you still feel empty inside.
Maybe you feel that way sometimes. But when it seems that
nothing will cheer you up, turn to Jesus!

Jesus might not bring you a gift or make a funny face, but He'll
make you glad on the inside where it really counts. He can
change your perspective, because where He is, there is joy. Ask
Jesus to come and cheer up your heart. Give Him your
depression—your ashes—and let Him crown you with beauty.

I am glad, and I want you to be glad . . . not a fake-smile kind of
glad, but a deep-down-in-your-heart kind of glad.

Your Joy-Giver,
>God

A PROVEN FRIEND

My command is this: Love each other as I have loved you. Greater love has no one than this, that he lay down his life for his friends.

| John | 15:12-13 |

Dear Child,

>Do you have a best friend? Would you be willing to die for her or him? It's easy to say yes now, but what if someone had a gun to your head? Is there anyone in your life that you love so much you would die for them?

Jesus loves you that much, and to prove it, He actually *did* die for you. He died so that you would know He was your friend. Jesus is not just some spooky, holy, faraway guy with white robes and a beard. He's Someone Who wants to call you friend. You can talk to Him when you pray and tell Him about your day. You can tell Him what you like and what you don't like.

Get to know Jesus as your friend. Hang out with My Son. He's great company!

Jesus' Dad,
>God

== == ==   == == == == == == == == ==

RESPECT HIS HOLY HOUSE

You realize, don't you, that you are the temple
of God, and God himself is present in you?
No one will get by with vandalizing God's
temple, you can be sure of that.

| 1 Corinthians | 3:16-17 THE MESSAGE |

Dear Child of Mine,

>Your body is the holy place where My Son wants to live. He
only needs to be invited in, and He will make His home in you.

Once Jesus has moved in, He will want you to treat His house
(your body) as a place of honor. Just like you wouldn't want
someone walking into your house and throwing a lot of trash
around or writing on the walls, He won't want you or anyone else
treating your body with disrespect because He will be living
there. What you eat, drink, read, watch, and think about—all of
those go into My Son's home.

Make sure that you only invite in what will please Him. And make
sure your friends understand the house rules, too! Welcome
Jesus home today!

Your Creator,
>God

== == ==   == == == == == == == == ==

I AM HERE FOR YOU

He was despised and rejected by men,
a man of sorrows, and familiar with suffering.
Like one from whom men hide their faces
he was despised, and we esteemed him not.

| Isaiah | 53:3 |

Child of Mine,

>Maybe you think Jesus never got His feelings hurt. Maybe you
think He didn't even have feelings like you do because He was God.

Well, He was God, but He was also a human being. So He felt
hurt and rejected when people were cruel to Him. I'll tell you
something else: When people hurt Him, they were hurting Me,
too. It's the same with you. When people hurt you, they hurt Me.
When your heart is breaking, My heart is breaking.

So on one of those really crummy days when you feel like your
heart's been kicked around like a football and nobody cares—
remember, I care. Come to Me, and I'll comfort you just like I
comforted Jesus. I am here for you.

Your Comforter,
>God

== == ==   == == == == == == == ==

LET LOVE TAKE OVER

There is no room in love for fear. Well-formed
love banishes fear. Since fear is crippling, a fearful
life—fear of death, fear of judgment—
is one not yet fully formed in love.

1 John 4:18 | THE MESSAGE

My Child,

>Fear is one of the most destructive, paralyzing emotions in the world. It can keep you from fulfilling your dreams—doing the things that will make you the happiest.

Fear hits different people in different ways. Some people fear failure; some fear success. Some fear dying, and others fear living. Some fear the criticism that keeps them from moving forward toward their dreams.

Let Me tell you a secret that will rid your life of fear. A heart that is filled with love has no room for fear. As My love rushes in and takes over, fear has to let go and find another place to hang out. So let Me fill you with My love and watch fear disappear. Love is My specialty!

Love always,
>God

== == ==   == == == == == == == == ==

JESUS HAS DESIGNS ON YOUR LIFE

It's in Christ that we find out who we are and what
we are living for. Long before we first heard of Christ
and got our hopes up, he had his eye on us,
had designs on us for glorious living.

Ephesians | **1:11 THE MESSAGE**

My Child,

>When you enroll in college, you take an interest and aptitude
test to find out what subject you should major in. Those tests
can be helpful, but the truth is, you could learn those things (and
a whole lot more) just by talking to My Son.

Long before you had even heard of Jesus, He knew all about
you. He knew who you would grow up to be. He knew what you'd
be most interested in and what you'd be good at. He even had a
plan for what part He wanted you to play in life. You can ignore
that plan if you want to, but if you do, you'll be missing out on the
fun and adventure of discovering your true purpose for living.

Jesus wants to lead you into this adventure. How about it? Are
you ready to follow?

Your Guide,
>God

== == ==   == == == == == == == == ==

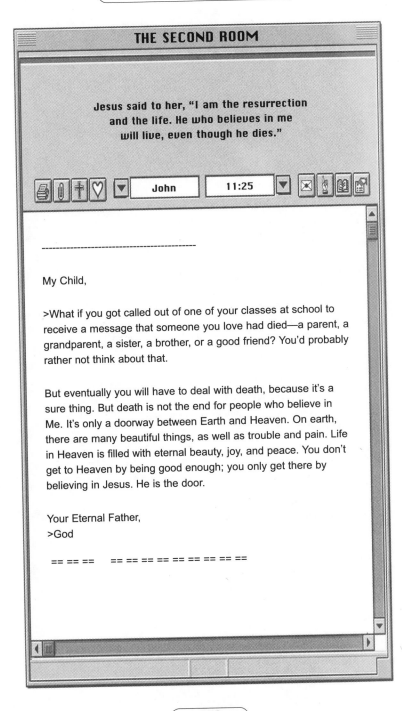

THE SECOND ROOM

Jesus said to her, "I am the resurrection
and the life. He who believes in me
will live, even though he dies."

John   11:25

My Child,

>What if you got called out of one of your classes at school to
receive a message that someone you love had died—a parent, a
grandparent, a sister, a brother, or a good friend? You'd probably
rather not think about that.

But eventually you will have to deal with death, because it's a
sure thing. But death is not the end for people who believe in
Me. It's only a doorway between Earth and Heaven. On earth,
there are many beautiful things, as well as trouble and pain. Life
in Heaven is filled with eternal beauty, joy, and peace. You don't
get to Heaven by being good enough; you only get there by
believing in Jesus. He is the door.

Your Eternal Father,
>God

THE GIFT THAT CHANGES YOU

For it is by grace you have been saved,
through faith—and this not from
yourselves, it is the gift of God.

| Ephesians | | 2:8 | |

Dear Child,

>What's holding you back from accepting My free gift of a new
life? Do you think that if you accept, you'll have to change
yourself and be perfect from now on? That I'll be mad if you ever
mess up?

That's not the deal. In fact, it's totally backwards. What I'm
offering you is a gift. A gift is free. You can't earn it with your
good behavior. You don't change to earn the gift. You accept the
gift, and it changes you!

What exactly is the gift? What is this new life all about? It's
about forgiveness, freedom, and friendship with Me. It's about a
deeper happiness than you have ever experienced and an inner
feeling of calm and peace that you can't find anywhere else.
Believe in Me. Receive your free gift!

Your Heavenly Father,
>God

== == ==   == == == == == == == == ==

BE A JANITOR?

For he who is least among you all—he is the greatest.

| 🖨 📎 ✝ ♡ ▼ | Luke | 9:48 | ▼ ✉ ✍ 📖 🏠 |

My Child,

>Titles, accomplishments, and awards don't impress Me. As a matter of fact, I'm often more impressed by the heart of the janitor than I am by the president of a company. People at the top sometimes *use* others instead of *serving* others.

But if you're a janitor, whom are you going to use? As a janitor, you're always serving others. You have to come to work every day willing to clean up other people's messes. It's that type of serving that impresses Me. My Son could have come to earth as a king or a president, but He came as a servant.

When I see someone willing to serve others, I'll put them on top, because I know I can trust them.

Your Servant,
>God

== == ==   == == == == == == == == ==

TAKE THAT RISK

Jesus gave them this answer: "I tell you the truth, the Son can do nothing by himself; he can do only what he sees his Father doing, because whatever the Father does the Son also does.

John **5:19**

Dear Child of Mine,

>Lots of people believe that Jesus must have had some kind of big game plan mapped out for His life—that every day He woke up and moved smoothly from point A to point B to point C. Wrong!

Jesus didn't know what He was going to do from one minute to the next! He just kept His eyes on Me, and I gave Him the day's agenda. He woke up each morning, never sure what the day would bring, but willing to listen to Me and do things My way. He knew the Scriptures backwards and forwards.

I want the same kind of life for you, so start by reading My Word. Practice keeping your eyes on Me, and when I show you what to do, take that risk and just do it! Trust Me. My dreams for you are even greater than what you could ever ask or think.

Your Life-Planner,
>God

== == ==   == == == == == == == == ==

I'VE GOT A PRESENT FOR YOU

You will fill me with joy in your presence, with eternal pleasures at your right hand.

| Psalm | 16:11 |

My Child,

>What gives you pleasure? For some, it's a close Superbowl game that goes down to the wire. For others, it's a quiet walk in the park enjoying the spring flowers, or buying the new live CD of their favorite band.

The pleasures of life make you glad to be alive. Now think about eternal pleasures—pleasures that last forever. Many of the world's pleasures get old after just a little while, like a week-old Christmas toy that's no longer any fun. But the pleasures I give never wear out.

Are you interested? Then take some time and get to know Me. The people who know Me are the ones who discover My everlasting pleasures.

Your Gift-Giver,
>God

JUST BE YOU

For you created my inmost being; you knit me
together in my mother's womb. I praise you
because I am fearfully and wonderfully made;
your works are wonderful, I know that full well.

| Psalm | 139:13–14 |

My Dear Child,

>Sometimes you don't like your looks and you blame Me. You
ask, "Why didn't you give me perfect skin like this person" or "a
perfect body like that person?"

You're letting magazines and movies define good looks for you.
You're listening to the lies of a money-hungry world. They want
to sell you skin treatments and diet books, so they convince you
something's wrong with you. Remember when Jesus found
money changers doing business in the temple? He went ballistic!

You are the temple in which My Spirit wants to make a home,
and it infuriates Me to see these money grubbers trying to sell
you a lie. I'm the One Who thought you up, and I love what I
made! You're the only you I've got. So just be you!

Your Creator,
>God

== == ==   == == == == == == == == ==

LET'S TALK TODAY

Before they call I will answer; while they are still speaking I will hear.

Isaiah 65:24

Dear Child,

>Prayer is not a process of trying to talk Me into doing something that I don't want to do. Prayer is realizing how willing I am to be involved in your life and how excited I am about involving you in Mine.

The moment you admit in prayer that you've been wrong, I forgive you. In prayer, I can encourage you when you're down and show you the way when you're lost. I can give you courage to face your fears, and I can bend down to dry your tears.

Can't you tell by now how much I want to talk with you? In fact, I'm listening for your prayers day and night. I'm already answering your call while it's still just a thought in your head! Let's talk today.

Your Friend Who Listens,
>God

== == ==   == == == == == == == == ==

I LOVE YOU FOREVER

Though the mountains be shaken and the hills
be removed, yet my unfailing love for you will not
be shaken nor my covenant of peace be removed,"
says the LORD, who has compassion on you.

		Isaiah		54:10		

Dear Child,

>I have chosen you to be Mine. I want to have a relationship
with you. Even if you turn from Me—even if you hate Me—I will
still love you.

Your attitude and behavior don't change My love for you. If you
turn from Me, or cut yourself off from Me, I still want to be with
you. It's like when you turn off the faucet. Does the water just
disappear out of the pipe? No, it stays there waiting for you to
turn on the faucet again. I'm like that water. I'm here waiting. I
want you as My child. No disobedience or rebellion on your part
can change that.

I have chosen you, and I will never reject you. Please don't cut
yourself off from My love.

Your Faithful Father,
>God

== == ==   == == == == == == == == ==

WHAT ABOUT EVIL?

Yet the Lord longs to be gracious to you;
he rises to show you compassion.
For the Lord is a God of justice.
Blessed are all who wait for him!

| Isaiah | 30:18 |

My Child,

>Why is there evil in the world? If I'm so powerful, then why do I let bad things happen? It's like this—I've chosen to let people make their own decisions, and many people have decided to go against Me.

Whenever people set themselves against Me and My goodness, that's evil. But I hate evil, and I hate it when people are hurt. The good news is, when people decide to obey Me, to let Me be in control, those people receive My justice.

Has someone done evil to you? I didn't do it. I want to protect you and love you and bless you. Choose Me, and your life will be better, even though you live in a world full of evil. In the end, I will destroy all evil. Until then, choose My way. I love you so much.

The Lord of Justice,
>God

== == ==   == == == == == == == == ==

AN ADDED BONUS

> That's my parting gift to you. Peace.
> I don't leave you the way you're used
> to being left. . . . So don't be upset.

| John 14:27 | THE MESSAGE |

My Child,

>Most people live with chaos and conflict in their lives: outside conflicts with other people and situations, and inside conflicts between different opinions and ideas in their own heads.

Jesus wants to give you peace. When you receive His love, His peace is an added bonus. When you embrace His friendship, you'll be able to set Him, like the sun, in the center of your personal solar system. Then all of the chaotic struggles and conflicts tend to quiet down. All of the questions untangle themselves. All of the things you care about line up and revolve around Jesus, like planets pulled into the orbit of His grace. And He will give you peace.

Peace always,
>God

== == ==   == == == == == == == == ==

LET MY WORDS BECOME ACTIONS

If you love me, show it by doing what I've told you.

John 14:15 | THE MESSAGE

My Child,

>When you begin to love Me—really love Me—something will happen in your life. You'll fall in love with My words, and My words will show up in your actions.

All the secrets I've shared, the stories I've told, the mysteries I've explained, the guidance I've given will affect you in a daily way. Every aspect of your life will be touched—your decisions, your friendships, your attitudes, and your faith. My words will become like a software program that is downloaded into your heart and mind, and you'll begin to respond to what I've said as easily as a computer responds to the program it's operating.

Life is exciting when My words affect your actions! Let My words make a difference.

Your Programmer,
>God

== == ==   == == == == == == == == ==

I WILL MEET ALL YOUR NEEDS

I have learned to be content whatever
the circumstances.... I can do everything
through him who gives me strength.

| Philippians | 4:11,13 |

Dear Child,

>Contentment is a valuable commodity. Some people have
boats, cars, big houses, and money, but they can't find
contentment. What good is all that stuff if they aren't satisfied
with it?

Contentment is something that only I can give. Paul, one of My
children, spent a lot of his life in jail. But even there, Paul was
content because he knew this truth: "Jesus gives me all I need."
Despite his circumstances, Paul knew that Jesus would take
care of him.

Trust Me to meet your needs, and you will always be content.
Only I can meet your needs . . . and I will.

The Giver of Contentment,
>God

== == ==   == == == == == == == == ==

FRESH INGREDIENTS MAKE THE DIFFERENCE

Summing it all up, friends, I'd say you'll do best
filling your minds . . . [with] things true, noble,
reputable, authentic, compelling, gracious—
the best, not the worst; the beautiful, not
the ugly; things to praise, not things to curse.

Philippians **4:8 THE MESSAGE**

Dear Child,

>Any good cook will tell you that the success of a dish depends on
fresh ingredients. Try making a delicious stew out of rancid meat
and rotten vegetables, and no matter what spices you add or how
long you cook it, you're going to end up with a terrible tasting mess.

Instead, when you begin with good, fresh vegetables and fresh,
prime meat and add the right combination of spices, you'll want a
second helping! The same principle applies to your life. If you fill
your head with rotten ingredients, like violence, hatred, and other
trash, you're going to cook up a life that's far from delicious.

Use My favorite recipe: Fill your mind with what is true, beautiful,
and good; add My love, then enjoy the best life you've ever tasted!

Your Chef,
>God

== == ==   == == == == == == == == ==

SH-H-H-H, SLOW DOWN

This is what the Sovereign LORD, the Holy One
of Israel, says: "In repentance and
rest is your salvation, in quietness
and trust is your strength."

| Isaiah | 30:15 |

Dear Child of Mine,

>Repentance is just a fancy word that means "to turn around." It
literally means "to change your mind."

My advice is to change your mind about all the busyness in your
life. Most people think the more they plan and the more they do,
the safer and stronger they will be. I see it differently. I want you
to slow down and take time to be quiet. Rest and trust Me, and
I'll help you to be strong and successful anyway. That doesn't
mean that you never have to plan or take action, but it does
mean that if all you do is plan and try, you're missing out on My
best for you.

Taking time out to be with Me during a busy day is always a
good idea. As you wait on Me, I'll give you the strength you
need. Slow down a little!

Your Advisor,
>God

== == ==   == == == == == == == == ==

YOU'LL THANK ME LATER

**My son, do not make light of the Lord's discipline,
and do not lose heart when he rebukes you,
ecause the Lord disciplines those he loves,
and he punishes everyone he accepts as a son.**

Hebrews 12:5-6

My Child,

>Think about a marathon runner and his coach. Some days the runner doesn't feel like running, but the coach will motivate the runner to run anyway. The runner might hate his coach during the training period, but on race day, after the victory is won, both runner and coach will rejoice.

I'm your Coach for life. I'll challenge and discipline you in preparation for victory. I have a race for you to run. There are things I want you to accomplish. I value you and your success. I correct you because I love you, and I want you to win. Hang in there and trust Me.

Your Coach,
>God

YOU CAN BE LIKE JESUS

For from the beginning God decided that
those who came to him . . . should become
like his Son, so that his Son would
be the First, with many brothers.

Romans | **8:29 TLB**

Dear Child,

>Who do you look like in your earthly family? Your brother, your
mother, your sister, your dad? Did you know that when you are
adopted as a child into My spiritual family, you resemble your big
brother, Jesus?

Not physically, of course, but every day your heart, your
thoughts, and your actions remind Me of Him. And the longer
you're around Him, the more you act like Him. I want you to care
about hurting people with broken hearts and those who are
weaker than yourself . . . just like He did. Believe Me, I know it's
hard. His goodness is impossible to imitate on your own.

But when I fill you with My Holy Spirit, you will have the power to
live and love like Jesus. Let Me make you more like Him. I can
do it!

Your Loving Father,
>God

== == ==   == == == == == == == == ==

TRUST ME, NO MATTER WHAT

> If we are thrown into the blazing furnace,
> the God we serve is able to save us from it. . . . But
> even if he does not, we want you to know,
> O king, that we will not serve your gods.

Daniel 3:17–18

My Child,

>Once a king tried to force three young men to worship him, but they wouldn't do it. Why? I told them not to worship anyone but Me.

Well, the king got angry and decided to burn them to death. So the three young men told the king, "God is going to save us, but even if He doesn't, we're still going to obey Him." The end of the story is, I did save them. But the point of the story is, they were willing to worship Me whether I saved them or not.

I'm still looking for young people who'll take a stand for Me like those three did. I'll know that you are truly intense about Me when you decide to obey Me, not because of what I can do for you, but simply because you love Me. I love you, too.

Your Deliverer,
>God

== == ==   == == == == == == == == ==

NOTHING IS IMPOSSIBLE

For nothing is impossible with God.

Luke	1:37

Dear Child of Mine,

>Are you going through something right now that seems totally impossible? The more you worry and stew about it, the more impossible it seems. Have you looked at it from every direction, figured it from every angle, tried everything humanly possible, and still you've struck out? Good!

I've been waiting for you to run out of human answers. Now is the time for faith—faith in Me and My strength. Now is the time to remember that I am with you right in the middle of this problem. And when I am with you, nothing is impossible!

I will bring unlimited possibilities into your "impossible" situations if only you trust Me. I won't let you down. I promise.

Powerfully yours,
>God

== == ==   == == == == == == == == ==

LOVE JESUS BY LOVING OTHERS

I tell you the truth, whatever you did for one of the least of these brothers of mine, you did for me.

| | | Matthew | | 25: 40 | | | |

My Child,

>Have you ever thought that if you could just see Jesus with your own eyes, it would be easier for you to believe in Him? Would it surprise you to know that you *can* see Him? In fact you do—every day! You look right into His face, but you don't recognize Him.

He's the janitor at your school and the handicapped boy or girl who always feels left out. He's the teacher no one likes and the kid no one wants to eat lunch with. He's walking on the streets and riding in the traffic. He's the ragged woman with her shopping cart full of junk and the old man selling papers on the corner.

Jesus wears millions of disguises, and He wants you to look for Him in people's faces. If you want to love and serve Jesus . . . love and serve another person.

Jesus' Father,
>God

== == ==   == == == == == == == == ==

STRENGTH TO GET THE JOB DONE

He gives strength to the weary and increases the power of the weak.

Isaiah 40:29

Dear Child,

>Have you ever been worn out? Ever felt like you have forty-eight hours of homework to do, and only four hours in which to do it? When you're physically and mentally exhausted, call on Me. I can cut your workload in half!

If you'll stop and listen to Me, I'll show you shortcuts and more efficient ways to get the job done. Some of the things you're doing might not even need to be done. Most of all, after spending time with Me, you'll be strengthened in your mind and body. My love is like a spiritual vitamin that refreshes and wakes you up. Five minutes with Me could save you hours of work.

So when you feel like you just can't go on . . . don't! Take a break and let Me renew your strength.

Your Rejuvenator,
>God

== == ==   == == == == == == == == ==

GIVE WITH ENTHUSIASM

Then a poor widow came by and dropped in two small copper coins. . . . [Jesus] remarked, "this poor widow has given more than all . . . [the rich] combined. For they have given a little of what they didn't need, but she . . . has given everything she has."

Luke　21:2-4 TLB

My Child,

>Rich people who try to buy My approval by throwing money at Me don't impress Me one bit. If a millionaire only gives Me a hundred dollars, it doesn't excite Me much. That's like pocket change to the rich. But if a really poor person gives Me ten bucks, I love their gift, because I know how much they sacrificed to give.

Let Me share a secret with you. If you want to know what's really important to most people, take a look at how they spend their time and money. The most important thing to Me is not the amount of the gift, but the generous spirit behind the gift and the wholehearted, cheerful way it's given. I want your whole heart.

Enthusiastically,
>God

== == ==　== == == == == == == == ==

JESUS CAN STILL CALM STORMS

He got up, rebuked the wind and said to the waves, "Quiet! Be still!" Then the wind died down and it was completely calm.

Mark 4:39

Dear Child of Mine,

>One night when Jesus and His friends were out at sea, a fierce storm came up and everybody panicked . . . everybody except Jesus.

Jesus was zonked out in the back of the boat taking a nap. That didn't go over so well with His friends. They were majorly ticked at Him for sleeping through their big catastrophe. What did Jesus do? He stood up and had a word with the wind and the waves. "Quiet! Chill!" He said, and the storm died down.

Jesus still does awesome things like that. No matter what kind of storm you're caught up in, talk to Jesus about it. Tell Him what you need. He can speak to the circumstances in your life, and you'll know His peace. Let Jesus calm your storms.

Peacefully yours,
>God

== == ==   == == == == == == == == ==

AND HE HUFFED, AND HE PUFFED

I have set the LORD always before me. Because he is at my right hand, I will not be shaken.

| 🖨 📎 ✝ ♡ ▼ | Psalm | 16:8 | ▼ ⊠ |

My Child,

>Do you know the story of the "Three Little Pigs"? (I know you're mature, but bear with Me.) The two foolish pigs built their houses out of straw and wood. Those houses were NOT big-bad-wolf proof. But the wise pig built his house out of bricks, and the wolf couldn't blow that one down.

Now the wise pig wasn't trusting in his masonry skills, and he wasn't trusting in his own strength. He was trusting in one thing— the sturdiness of the brick. If you think that you're clever enough to defeat the devil with your own strength, he will eat you up.

There is only one thing that will keep the devil from defeating you . . . putting Me first in your life. Then, like the wise pig, you can laugh at the big bad wolf. So if I were you, I'd trust in Me.

Your Fortress,
>God

== == ==   == == == == == == == == ==

GOLD THAT WON'T TARNISH

All good athletes train hard. They do it for a
gold medal that tarnishes and fades.
You're after one that's gold eternally.

| 1 Corinthians | 9:25 THE MESSAGE |

Dear Child,

>When you train to win a race or a championship for your team,
you put in lots of time and practice. You schedule workouts and
concentrate on strategy sessions with your coach. You sweat—
a lot.

If it all pans out the way you hope, you'll be called to the victor's
stand at an awards ceremony. You'll experience the satisfaction
of having your hard work pay off. But aside from a feeling of
pride, all you'll have to show for it is a tin medal or trophy that's
destined to tarnish.

The medal you're training for as you live this life for Me is made
of gold that never tarnishes. And the satisfaction you will feel as
you enter My Kingdom will come from hearing Me say, "Well
done, good and faithful servant!" So go for the gold!

Your Rewarder,
>God

== == ==   == == == == == == == == ==

LEAVE THE DRIVING TO ME

Anyone who intends to come with me has to let me lead. You're not in the driver's seat; I am. Don't run from suffering; embrace it. Follow me and I'll show you how. Self-help is no help at all. Self-sacrifice is the way . . . to finding . . . your true self.

Matthew | **16:24-25 THE MESSAGE**

My Dear Child,

>I'm about to give you a hard assignment. Take your hands off of the handlebars. This bicycle (your life) only needs one driver, and I want you to leave it to Me. If you can do that, I promise you the ride of your life!

We will pedal together through surprising and difficult places. You'll sometimes say to Me, "No, Father, this is too scary!" But I'll just answer, "Hold on, and trust Me. This is the way." What you're signing up for is not a self-help program. There won't be any New Year's resolutions, or turning over a new leaf, or patching up your old self. The real you and I are going on a great adventure, and I'm the only One Who's got the map. So hang on!

Your Guide,
>God

== == ==   == == == == == == == == ==

I'M AN EXPERT ON LOVING YOU

"The most important [commandment],"
answered Jesus, "is . . . Love the Lord your
God with all your heart and with all your soul
and with all your mind and with all your strength.'
The second is this: 'Love your neighbor as yourself.'
There is no commandment greater than these."

| | Mark | 12:29-31 | |

My Child,

>Somebody asked Jesus to name My most important rule. He said it was to love God whole-heartedly. Then He added that the second most important rule was to love other people as much as you love yourself.

Jesus was right. But if you don't love yourself, how can you love others? If you are always finding fault with yourself, constantly beating yourself up over every little thing, you'll probably act the same way with others. So step one in loving others is learning to love yourself.

I wish you could see the good things I see in you. I'm so proud of you! Let Me teach you how to love yourself. (I'm an expert on loving you!) Then you can get on with the business of loving others.

Your Father,
>God

== == ==   == == == == == == == == ==

FORGIVE AND LET IT GO

Then Peter came to Jesus and asked, "Lord, how many times shall I forgive my brother when he sins against me? Up to seven times?" Jesus answered, "I tell you, not seven times, but seventy-seven times.

Matthew   18:21-22

Dear Child,

>Is there anyone in your life who drives you up a wall? Have you ever felt like giving up on that relationship? Well, I'm asking you to hang in there. Give that person another chance.

After all, I never give up on you. I forgive you again and again and again. If I cut you infinite slack, why can't you do the same for others? I want you to rely on My forgiveness for you, but I also want you to demonstrate that same kind of forgiveness to everyone in your life. I know it's hard to forgive sometimes, but I'll help you.

So right now if there's anyone who comes to mind who you need to forgive (again), here's what I want you to do. Forgive them and move on. You'll be glad you did.

Your Forgiving Father,
>God

== == ==   == == == == == == == == ==

I'M RIGHT HERE

Seek the Lord while he may be found;
call on him while he is near.

Isaiah | 55:6

My Child,

>Where do you think I live? Heaven? You're right, but I also live on earth through My Holy Spirit. I'm at work all around you, helping and advising My kids.

But I'm even closer than that. If you're a Christian, I live inside of you. I feel what you feel. So when you need Me, you don't have to look far. There was a time in history when My people had to go into a tent or a temple to meet Me. Not any more.

Because Jesus died on the cross, now I can live inside of you. You're My temple now. I know your every thought. You can call on Me any time. I'm right here, as close as your heartbeat.

Your Heavenly Father,
>God

== == ==   == == == == == == == == ==

IT'S WORTH THE WAIT

**That's why I don't think there's any
comparison between the present hard times
and the coming good times. The created world
itself can hardly wait for what's coming next.**

| | | | | | Romans 8: 18-19 | | THE MESSAGE | | | | | |

Dear Child of Mine,

>What if you knew that an incredible, never-ending party had
been planned and your name was on the guest list? But before
the band could start, before the refreshments could be served,
before the party could even begin, there would be some really
rough days.

That's a pretty good picture of what's going on right now in the
world. All the bad stuff—the crime and poverty—grieves Me. All
the international struggles—the wars and world hunger—break
My heart. But I want you to know that for those who follow Me,
the troubling times won't last forever. Soon, they'll be history!

That never-ending party is just around the corner. It's going to be
more amazing than anything you've ever imagined! So hang on
through the tough times. There's a party in your future.

Your Host,
>God

== == ==   == == == == == == == == ==

GIVE TO THE COLD AND THE HUNGRY

The crowd [asked Jesus], "What do you want
us to do?" "If you have two coats," he replied,
"give one to the poor. If you have extra food,
give it away to those who are hungry."

Luke 3: 10–11 TLB

My Child,

>All that you own is a gift from Me. Don't squirrel it away just for
yourself. Share what I've given to you with others who are in
need. They are so hungry—hungry for food and affirmation.
They are so cold—cold as they sleep in parked cars or under
bridges, cold from the apathy they see in people's eyes.

You are My hands and My heart in a world desperately in need of
warmth and affection. But you don't have to just rely on your own
strength to make a difference in their lives. As I have given to you,
so I will give to others through you. Keep your eyes and ears,
along with your heart, open. We have work to do, together!

Your Provider,
>God

== == ==   == == == == == == == == ==

IT'S AN INSIDE JOB

The LORD does not look at the things man looks at. Man looks at the outward appearance, but the LORD looks at the heart.

1 Samuel | 16:7

My Child,

>The world you live in is much more interested in what you look like on the outside than what's on the inside of you. I'm just the opposite. I check out your heart.

I see the scars where you've been wounded by mean words and bad attitudes. I see your hopes—the ones you're afraid to reach for—and the dreams that haven't come true.

But if you're willing to let Me move in with you, I'll bring Jesus and all the power of the Holy Spirit with Me. I want to make you stronger and more positive. Believe Me, when We move in, good things will begin to happen. The three of Us work together as a team to heal the hidden part of you. This is an inside job!

Your Healer,
>God

== == ==   == == == == == == == == ==

THE GOD WHO FORGETS

**As far as sunrise is from sunset,
[The Lord] has separated us from our sins.**

| Psalm 103:13 | THE MESSAGE |

Dear Child,

>Here's something that might surprise you. Even though I'm the smartest Person ever, I have a bad memory when it comes to one thing: When you tell Me you're sorry for all the bad stuff you've done and decide to stop doing it, I can't even remember what it was that you did wrong.

I'm serious. I forget it; it's vaporized! I don't file that stuff away to pull out later and rub it in your face. Actually, you probably remember what you did wrong better than I do. I don't want to remember the bad things you've done. I'd rather start over with you and move on.

Is there anything you want to get off your chest? Tell Me. I'm just waiting to forgive you and make it disappear.

Forgetfully yours,
>God

== == ==   == == == == == == == == ==

JESUS KNOWS WHAT YOU'RE GOING THROUGH

We don't have a priest who is out of touch
with our reality. He's been through weakness
and testing, experienced it all—all but the sin.

Hebrews 4:15 | **THE MESSAGE**

Dear Child of Mine,

>You might picture Jesus as wearing a halo and hanging out in
Heaven with a bunch of angels. It's true that He lives in Heaven
now, but don't ever forget that He was a real flesh-and-blood
human being just like you when He lived in Israel.

In fact, He experienced a lot of the same things you do. He felt
everything you feel. He laughed and cried. He got homesick. He
got hungry, angry, lonely, and tired. He felt hurt and
disappointment. He was happy and excited. He celebrated. He
struggled and was tired, troubled, and tempted.

He never wants you to forget that whatever you're going
through now, He's been there before you, and He wants to help.
Jesus understands.

Your Loving Father,
>God

== == ==   == == == == == == == == ==

HIS PEOPLE KNOW HIS VOICE

**My sheep listen to my voice;
I know them, and they follow me.**

| | John | 10:27 | |

My Child,

>Do you ever wonder what Jesus would be doing if He were alive in the world today? He would be right in the middle of the people who need Him most, listening to their problems and teaching them to know Me.

He would be helping them live joyful, peaceful, purposeful lives. He would help in your neighborhood and in nursing homes, hospitals, and homeless shelters. He might teach in your school or Sunday school if He were alive today.

Guess what! He *is* alive, and He's in all of those places doing all of those things. He's working through people who believe in Him— people who are filled with His Spirit and equipped with His love.

Have you been listening for His voice? Can you hear Him calling you to be one of His people? His kids know His voice and follow Him.

Jesus' Dad,
>God

== == ==   == == == == == == == == ==

LET ME HELP YOU CHANGE

For what I do is not the good I want to do;
no, the evil I do not want to do—this
I keep on doing. What a wretched man I am!
Who will rescue me from this body of death?
Thanks be to God—through Jesus Christ our Lord!

Romans 7:19, 24–25

My Child,

>Have you ever promised yourself that you would change? It's so easy to make that promise and so hard to carry it out.

Does this sound familiar? You wake up and before you're even out of bed, you've decided, "Today is going to be different. Today I'm not going to lose my temper," or "Today I'm going to get all my homework done before bedtime," or "Today I'm not going to smoke pot," or "pig out," or "give my mom a hard time." But before the day is over, you've blown it again. Though you're trying to do right, you're trapped in a cycle of doing wrong.

If this is your life, don't give up. You're not alone. My Son and I are with you. We can help you change from the inside out. Let us help.

Your Life Changer,
>God

== == ==   == == == == == == == == ==

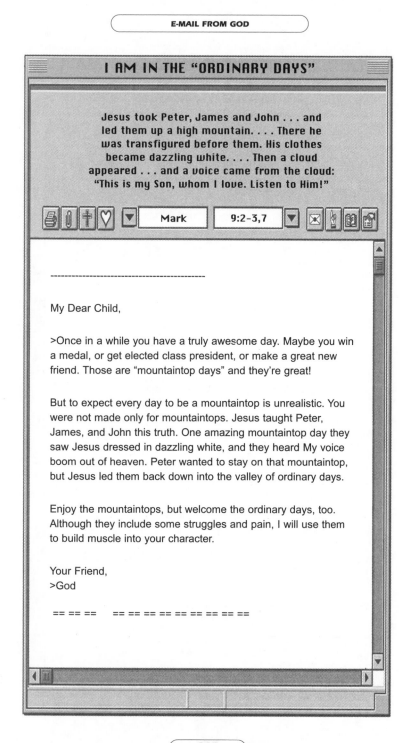

I AM IN THE "ORDINARY DAYS"

Jesus took Peter, James and John . . . and led them up a high mountain. . . . There he was transfigured before them. His clothes became dazzling white. . . . Then a cloud appeared . . . and a voice came from the cloud: "This is my Son, whom I love. Listen to Him!"

Mark | **9:2–3,7**

My Dear Child,

>Once in a while you have a truly awesome day. Maybe you win a medal, or get elected class president, or make a great new friend. Those are "mountaintop days" and they're great!

But to expect every day to be a mountaintop is unrealistic. You were not made only for mountaintops. Jesus taught Peter, James, and John this truth. One amazing mountaintop day they saw Jesus dressed in dazzling white, and they heard My voice boom out of heaven. Peter wanted to stay on that mountaintop, but Jesus led them back down into the valley of ordinary days.

Enjoy the mountaintops, but welcome the ordinary days, too. Although they include some struggles and pain, I will use them to build muscle into your character.

Your Friend,
>God

== == ==   == == == == == == == == ==

THE CROSS IS POWER

For the message of the cross is foolishness to those who are perishing, but to us who are being saved it is the power of God.

1 Corinthians   1:18

Dear Child,

>My Son Jesus was never elected king. For the last three years of His life, He was homeless and jobless. In the end, all His friends left Him, and the government killed Him like an outlaw.

Does it make sense to worship someone like Jesus? Does it seem reasonable? If you don't know My Son, you probably don't get it. If Jesus is a stranger to you, the cross will seem pretty weird.

But once you know Him, you'll begin to know His power. You'll realize that the cross is where Jesus died so that you could have a relationship with Me. The cross is where Jesus defeated your enemy, the devil. The cross is where Jesus displayed My love for you and earned a place for you in My family. Do you get it yet?

Your Father,
>God

== == ==   == == == == == == == == ==

LET ME BE YOUR DEFENDER

**Though I walk in the midst of trouble,
you preserve my life; you stretch out your
hand against the anger of my foes,
with your right hand you save Me.**

Psalm 138: 7

My Child,

>It's a tough world out there. Believe Me, I know. Sometimes people or circumstances seem to gang up on you, and when they do, you may feel afraid. That's okay. I understand, and I care.

I want to help you cope with life. That's why I want you to call on Me. Tell Me your fears. I'll be right beside you in the midst of your struggles.

If I have to carry you, I will. I'll be your defender. I want to make a difference in your everyday life. So, don't be afraid.

Your Defender,
>God

== == ==   == == == == == == == == ==

YOU ARE NOT THE JUDGE

**Do not say, "I'll pay you back for this wrong!"
Wait for the LORD, and he will deliver you.**

| | Proverbs | 20:22 | |

Dear Child,

>I haven't asked you to be the Terminator or the Avenger. It's not your job to take revenge on every single person who's ever wronged you. I don't want you to judge every case and sit on every jury. I can do a much better job of defending you if you'll just step back and let Me handle it.

If someone does you wrong, talk to Me about it. Forgive that person, and leave the situation in My hands. I'll deal with the situation in a way that will be best for him or her.

Then once you've turned the job of judging over to Me, leave it there. Anger and bitterness will eat your lunch. Turn your enemies over to Me. I'll take care of them.

Your Defender,
>God

== == ==   == == == == == == == == ==

WHY DID JESUS SUFFER?

> But he was pierced for our transgressions,
> he was crushed for our iniquities; the
> punishment that brought us peace was upon
> him, and by his wounds we are healed.

Isaiah **53:5**

My Child,

>Jesus was intense. Roman soldiers whipped Him so much He almost bled to death. Then they made Him carry a huge beam of wood on which they later hung Him by driving nails through His hands and feet. There they left Him, suffering for hours on the cross until He finally died.

Why? Why did My Son let them torture Him in that horrible way? Because of His love for you. He made it possible for you to escape punishment for your wrongdoing. He made it possible for you to live forever in Heaven with us.

On the cross, Jesus earned eternal life for you. It was a trade-off. Take advantage of it!

The Father of the Crucified,
>God

== == ==   == == == == == == == == ==

RECEIVE THE GIFT OF THE CROSS

He used his servant body to carry our sins to the Cross so we could be rid of sin.

1 Peter 2:24 | THE MESSAGE

My Child,

>Even the most perfect person has done something that deserves a death sentence. There are times when you've been cruel, or greedy, or conceited, or jealous. Just like one drop of poison pollutes a glass of water, one small lie pollutes your life and separates you from Me. Even the smallest, white lie earns the death penalty.

But I loved you so much that I gave all the bad stuff you've done, big and little, to Jesus on the cross. He held it there for you because I asked Him to do it. The power of your wrongdoing died when He was crucified. So when you believe in Jesus, all that bad stuff you've done is forgiven and washed away. It's My gift to you for the cost of My Son's life. Your debt is cancelled forever.

Love,
>God

I'LL SUPPLY THE POWER

That energy is God's energy, an energy deep
within you, God himself willing and working
at what will give him the most pleasure.

Philippians **2:13 THE MESSAGE**

My Child,

>Suppose a ritzy country club hired you to mow the grass on
their huge golf greens. But then instead of giving you a power
mower, you were given a tiny pair of fingernail clippers to do the
job. Can you imagine how frustrated you would feel to find
yourself facing such an impossible task?

In the same way, it would be like Me designing you for lots of life
challenges and then failing to give you the power and vision you
would need for the job. Relax. When I give you an assignment, I
also provide you with the power to accomplish it. It's My power,
and believe Me, it's more than enough.

Your Helper,
>God

== == ==   == == == == == == == == ==

A SPIRIT-TO-SPIRIT FRIEND

[The Father will] provide you another Friend
so that you will always have someone with you.
This Friend is the Spirit of Truth. He will
remind you of all the things I have told you.

John 14:16-17,26   THE MESSAGE

Dear Child of Mine,

>Before Jesus left earth to return home to Me, He asked Me to give you a gift. He knew He could no longer be a face-to-face kind of friend. So He asked Me to give you a Spirit-to-spirit kind of friend.

This Spirit Friend—the Holy Spirit—is a little harder to relate to at first because He's invisible. But His friendship has one big plus. Jesus could only be in one place at a time, but His Spirit can be wherever you are all the time.

The Holy Spirit doesn't have to run alongside your car to keep up with you. He can travel inside you and be close to you anywhere and everywhere, constantly refilling you, refueling you, and reminding you of Jesus' love. He's awesome!

Jesus' Dad,
>God

== == ==   == == == == == == == == ==

LET ME STRENGTHEN YOUR FAITH

**If you have faith as small as a mustard seed,
you can say to this mountain, "Move from
here to there" and it will move.
Nothing will be impossible for you.**

| Matthew | 17:20 |

My Child,

>I know that sometimes you pray as hard as you know how and
things just don't turn out the way you prayed they would. Then
you wonder where I was all that time. Did I hear you? Of course
I did.

Although you can't see Me, I'm always here. I know life feels
unfair at times. But prayer doesn't work like a soda machine
where you drop in the change and out pops the can. Prayer
works on faith. When you're confused, bring Me the jumbled mix
of feelings you have inside, and I'll give you faith.

Faith doesn't take a detour around pain; it builds a road through
your pain. Faith doesn't make things easy, but it does give you
extra strength for hard times. Faith can move mountains, even
mountains like fear, loneliness, and hopelessness. Let Me
strengthen your faith.

Your Faithful Friend,
>God

== == ==   == == == == == == == == ==

LET JESUS SIGN THE CHECK

The prayer of a person living right with God is something powerful to be reckoned with.

| James 5:16 | THE MESSAGE |

Dear Child,

>One of the most powerful forces in the world is a prayer by one of My children who trusts in Jesus—a prayer prayed in His name.

Praying in His name is like writing a check and letting Jesus sign His name at the bottom. Believe Me, He won't sign His name to anything that He's not in favor of, and I certainly won't cash a check without His signature! When you pray, ask in faith. Anyone can rattle off some mindless prayer without any faith behind it. That's about as pointless as throwing a penny into a wishing well.

But the heartfelt prayer of a Christ-believer carries with it all the power of Jesus Himself. So pray in His name with faith, and watch Me work!

Your Prayer Partner,
>God

== == ==   == == == == == == == == ==

GET PHYSICAL

**Come, let us bow down in worship,
let us kneel before the LORD our Maker.**

Psalm 95:6

Dear Child,

>At a football game, when your team wins, you don't just sit there and think, "Wow, this is great." You get up out of your seat. You jump up and down and yell! You use your body to express what you feel.

So when you pray, you should use your whole body. Some of My best pray-ers get physical. They get totally involved. I want you to do the same when you pray to Me. Get where no one can see you and kneel down before Me. If you are thankful, sing to Me or dance in front of Me. Lift your hands. Yell if you feel like! I don't care. I like it!

It will put you in the right mood and help you reach out to Me. I will see, and hear, and answer your prayers. Don't be ashamed.

Your Loving Father,
>God

== == ==   == == == == == == == == ==

THE MOST CONVINCING SIGN

Let me give you a new command: Love one another. In the same way I loved you, you love one another. This is how everyone will recognize that you are My disciples—when they see the love you have for each other."

John 13:34-35 — THE MESSAGE

My Child,

>The most convincing sign of My existence is not the big, impressive churches that people build in My name. It's not the number of dressed-up people who show up there on Sunday mornings. It's not the crosses people wear around their necks or the Christian bumper stickers on their cars.

Churches, Sunday school clothes, crosses, and bumper stickers are only the icing on the cake, just as the gift wrap is not the gift. The most authentic sign that I really am Who I say I am and that you are Mine is your love.

When people who don't know Me encounter the life-changing love you have for others, they'll know right away that there's something special about you. They might even want to get in on it! So let your love show and your light shine!

Your Loving Father,
>God

== == ==   == == == == == == == == ==

I'LL NEVER LEAVE YOU ALONE

**My son, do not despise the LORD's discipline
and do not resent his rebuke because the
LORD disciplines those he loves, as
a father the son he delights in.**

Proverbs 3:11-12

My Child,

>Some people think discipline means abuse. But discipline,
done correctly, is an act of love. If a child is reaching out to stick
a fork in an electrical socket, a good father will slap the child's
hand and say, "No!" The father's not mad. He loves his child too
much to stand by and do nothing.

If a child needs discipline in order to grow up happy, then a loving
father will provide that discipline. Some kids have parents who
don't care, and they grow up wild. They never learn right from
wrong. They start running with the wrong crowd; they fight, steal,
and wind up in jail. Believe Me, I wouldn't discipline you if there
weren't a good reason. I love you too much to let you run wild.

Your Daddy,
>God

== == ==   == == == == == == == == ==

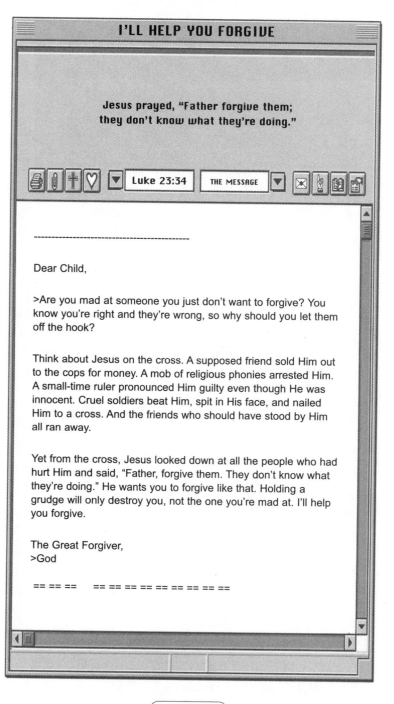

I'LL HELP YOU FORGIVE

Jesus prayed, "Father forgive them; they don't know what they're doing."

Luke 23:34 · THE MESSAGE

Dear Child,

>Are you mad at someone you just don't want to forgive? You know you're right and they're wrong, so why should you let them off the hook?

Think about Jesus on the cross. A supposed friend sold Him out to the cops for money. A mob of religious phonies arrested Him. A small-time ruler pronounced Him guilty even though He was innocent. Cruel soldiers beat Him, spit in His face, and nailed Him to a cross. And the friends who should have stood by Him all ran away.

Yet from the cross, Jesus looked down at all the people who had hurt Him and said, "Father, forgive them. They don't know what they're doing." He wants you to forgive like that. Holding a grudge will only destroy you, not the one you're mad at. I'll help you forgive.

The Great Forgiver,
>God

== == ==   == == == == == == == == ==

YOU ARE MY ADVERTISEMENT

**Because you are my help,
I sing in the shadow of your wings.**

| Psalm | 63:7 |

My Child,

>If I have done anything good for you, I want you to tell others about it. Don't keep it to yourself.

Maybe I answered a prayer, or maybe I protected you when you needed Me. If I've been good to you in any way, and you know it, then write a song or a poem about Me. Or just tell someone about Me. I want everyone to know how great I am and how much I love him or her. You're just the one to tell that person about Me.

Seeing a commercial for a new movie is not nearly as good as hearing your friend tell about it. You are My advertisement. Tell people about Me. Then they'll want to see for themselves. Share what I've done for you.

Your Heavenly Father,
>God

== == ==   == == == == == == == == ==

LET ME REFUEL YOUR LIFE

**And hope does not disappoint us, because
God has poured out his love into our hearts
by the Holy Spirit, whom he has given us.**

Romans   5:5

Dear Child,

>Trying to run your life without hope is like trying to run your car without gas; you won't get far. Sometimes it seems like the world has run out of hope. With all the hype and nonsense, people don't know what to believe in, so they don't believe in anything.

Some kids you know probably have learned to expect the worst. Maybe you've felt that way yourself. Well, even though it's easy to stop believing in other people and yourself, I can give you a reason to believe that your life is worth the effort—that the world is worth your best shot. Come and let Me refuel your life. Let Me fill you with hope. I've got plenty to spare!

The Hope that You Run On,
>God

== == ==   == == == == == == == == ==

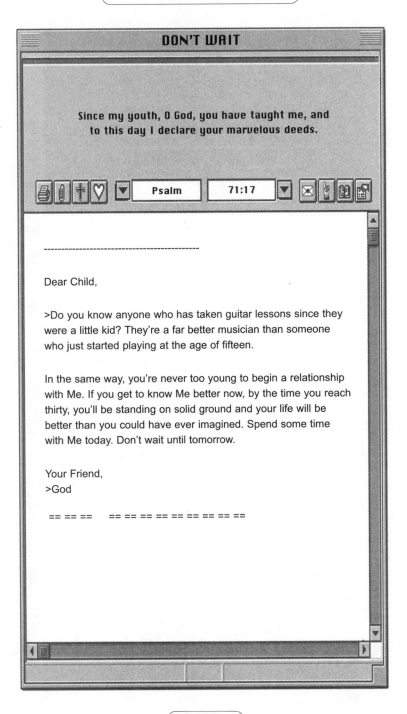

DON'T WAIT

Since my youth, O God, you have taught me, and to this day I declare your marvelous deeds.

| Psalm | 71:17 |

Dear Child,

>Do you know anyone who has taken guitar lessons since they were a little kid? They're a far better musician than someone who just started playing at the age of fifteen.

In the same way, you're never too young to begin a relationship with Me. If you get to know Me better now, by the time you reach thirty, you'll be standing on solid ground and your life will be better than you could have ever imagined. Spend some time with Me today. Don't wait until tomorrow.

Your Friend,
>God

== == ==   == == == == == == == == ==

I'LL SEE YOU AT THE PARTY

Everlasting joy will crown their heads.
Gladness and joy will overtake them,
and sorrow and sighing will flee away.

| Isaiah | 51:11 |

Dear Child,

>Have you ever felt like joy tracked you down, caught up with you, and jumped all over you? That probably doesn't describe your daily experience at school or work, does it?

But in Heaven, laughter, joy, singing, and fun are all regular activities. Just think—no sadness or tears. Some people say, "If Heaven is the only reason to become a Christian, that's pretty lame." But Heaven is an *excellent* reason to become a Christian.

The ones who are going to enjoy My eternal heavenly party are the ones who have asked My Son to rule their lives. Will I see you there? I hope so. Believe Me, Heaven is worth the wait!

Your Heavenly Host,
>God

== == ==   == == == == == == == == ==

LOVE IN ACTION

This is how we know what love is: Jesus Christ
laid down his life for us. . . . And this is his command:
to believe in the name of his Son, Jesus Christ,
and to love one another as he commanded us.

1 John | 3:16, 23

Dear Child of Mine,

>Jesus was love in action. You can see My love just by looking
at His life. He listened to people. He helped them, healed them,
and gave them hope.

But the most vivid picture of His love was His death on the
cross. Nobody took Jesus' life. He gave it up for you. The best
way to thank Him is to receive His love. Ask Him to love others
through you. He'll do it!

Pick out some people who really look like they need His love.
Don't try to love them with your own love. Let the love of Jesus
take over in you. You'll be surprised at the kindness and caring
that will come through you to others.

Your Loving Father,
>God

== == ==   == == == == == == == == ==

I CAN SET YOU FREE

For you did not receive a spirit that makes you a slave again to fear, but you received the Spirit of sonship. And by him we cry, "Abba, Father."

| | Romans | 8:15 | |

My Child,

>The Civil War was fought in the United States to end slavery. When the Union declared victory, all slaveholders were required to free their slaves.

My Son Jesus fought a war to end a different kind of slavery. When He died on the cross, He won a victory over fear, jealousy, hatred, and every other kind of bondage. After His victory, all those slaveholders were required to free their slaves, but a lot of people still haven't heard the war is over. They're still letting their old masters keep them tied up in knots.

What about you? Have you heard the news? You don't have to be a slave to anything anymore. Jesus has set you free!

Your Bondage Breaker,
>God

== == ==   == == == == == == == == ==

YOU CAN'T KEEP A GOOD MAN DOWN

We are hard pressed on every side, but not crushed; perplexed, but not in despair; persecuted, but not abandoned; struck down, but not destroyed.

| 2 Corinthians | 4:8-9 |

My Child,

>Paul was a Christian who lived a pretty difficult life while sharing the good news of Jesus. He was stoned several times and almost died. Paul spent years in prison, and finally, the Roman government cut off his head.

Sometimes, when you become a Christian, the circumstances of your life may seem to get worse. Then why become a Christian? Because when I live in you and you live for Me, you are able to more than overcome the circumstances of your life. While Paul was in jail, he sang songs. After being stoned, he went back to love the people who had stoned him.

I have the power to change your situation; but even better than that, I give you the power to *overcome* any situation. Now that's good news!

Your Strength,
>God

== == ==   == == == == == == == == ==

NO PROBLEM

"Not by might nor by power, but by
my Spirit," says the Lord Almighty.

Zechariah 4:6

My Child,

>Do you know the story of David and Goliath? David was this
young little guy with a slingshot. He was short and
inexperienced, but he was on My side. Goliath was a huge hunk
of a giant with a big spear. He was My enemy.

Using his slingshot, David hit Goliath in the head with a rock and
killed him. How did that rock land in just the right spot? How was
David able to stay calm enough to aim correctly? I helped him. I
won the battle for David because he trusted Me.

Are there things in your life that are just too big for you to overcome
by yourself? Pray, and I will help you win, too. I can do anything.

The Almighty,
>God

== == ==   == == == == == == == == ==

I WANT GOOD THINGS FOR YOU

And we know that in all things God works
for the good of those who love him, who
have been called according to his purpose.

| Romans | 8:28 |

My Child,

>Suppose you could invent a machine to turn bad stuff into good stuff. Insults would turn into compliments. Crummy days would turn into great days. Rain would turn into sunshine. You could probably sell your invention for big bucks and become a millionaire.

Well, I have an invention that turns bad into good. It's called redemption, and I can use it in the lives of people who love Me. I can take everything in your life, even the bad stuff, and make it work for good. Even the things that other people have meant to hurt you, I can use to bless you. Once you get a grip on this, you'll learn to say, "No matter how bad things look now, God can use this for good."

Your Father,
>God

== == ==   == == == == == == == == ==

THE TRUTH HAS A GREAT PAYOFF

Teach me your way, O Lord, and I will walk
in your truth; give me an undivided
heart, that I may fear your name.

Psalm   86:11

My Child,

>Sometimes it seems like the liars and crooks are the big
winners while the people who do right get the short end of the
stick. Some people don't even care about right and wrong. They
only care about not getting caught.

Maybe some of your friends have that attitude. They think you're
a loser if you try to be truthful and do the right thing. If that's
what your friends are like, you might need some new friends.
You see, I'm going to ask you to stand in a hard place—to value
the truth—to stand up for what's right even when it's not popular.

I want you to know the payoff for living a truthful life. It's an inner
peace and happiness that comes only from doing what's right in
My sight. It's a great way to live!

The Truth,
>God

== == ==   == == == == == == == == ==

A CHANCE AT REAL LIFE

This is how much God loved the world:
He gave his Son . . . so that no one need be
destroyed. . . . God didn't go to all the trouble of
sending his Son merely to point an accusing
finger, telling the world how bad it was.
He came to help, to put the world right again.

▼ John 3:16-17 | THE MESSAGE ▼

Dear Child,

>I don't get any kind of thrill out of catching you doing something
wrong. I'm not offering you a new life just to pull it back the
minute you reach out for it.

Just for you, I put together an elaborate plan and sent Jesus to
earth to rescue you. So I'm not waiting around just to pounce on
you when you do something wrong. His life was too precious for
Me to waste it on something as pointless as that.

My goal all along has been to show you My love and draw you
to Me—to heal your hurts and make you whole, and to give you
a chance at real life—life that lasts forever.

Your Father and Friend,
>God

== == ==   == == == == == == == == ==

WATCH JESUS

**But my eyes are fixed on you,
O Sovereign Lord; in you I take refuge.**

| Psalm | 141:8 |

Dear Child,

>How many of your friends quote the characters they see on television every day? Did you know that your mind stores away the things you hear or see? So if you watch people cursing, blowing up buildings, and shooting people, you've stored it all away in your mind. Whether you realize it or not, what you watch affects your behavior and attitudes in subtle ways.

But this truth can work for good, too. If you keep your eyes on Me, you'll become more like Me. I'm not on television, so how can you watch Me? You can read about Jesus in the Bible. Everything Jesus did was a reflection of Me. Read the book called John. It tells about the miracles Jesus did.

As you watch Jesus, you'll start acting more like Him. You'll catch His style. Then I can use you to do some of the things that He did. Check out My Son in the Bible. It's worth reading.

Your Father,
>God

== == ==   == == == == == == == == ==

WE'RE IN THIS TOGETHER

I said, "I do not know how to speak;
I am only a child." But the LORD said to me,
"Do not say, `I am only a child.' You must go
to everyone I send you to and say whatever
I command you. Do not be afraid of them, for I am
with you and will rescue you," declares the LORD.

| Jeremiah | 1:6-8 |

My Child,

>I know sometimes you feel inferior—like you don't have what it takes to do the things you've got to do. Sometimes you feel like everything is stacked against you and everyone else has more going for them than you do.

Lots of people have those feelings of inadequacy. But you've got a big advantage. You've got Me in your corner! I'm pulling for you. There are exciting, challenging things I want us to do together, and I'm going to be with you every step of the way, making sure you're ready to get the job done.

Don't let yourself get bummed out by other people and what they might think of you. Take their opinions with a grain of salt. I know you and what you can do. We're in this life together.

Your Encourager,
>God

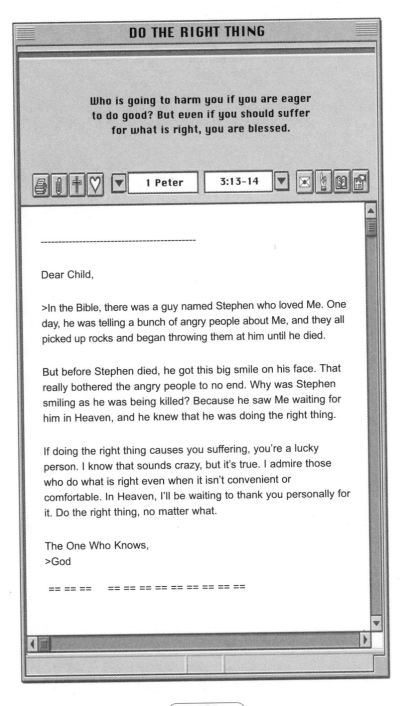

DO THE RIGHT THING

**Who is going to harm you if you are eager
to do good? But even if you should suffer
for what is right, you are blessed.**

1 Peter 3:13-14

Dear Child,

>In the Bible, there was a guy named Stephen who loved Me. One
day, he was telling a bunch of angry people about Me, and they all
picked up rocks and began throwing them at him until he died.

But before Stephen died, he got this big smile on his face. That
really bothered the angry people to no end. Why was Stephen
smiling as he was being killed? Because he saw Me waiting for
him in Heaven, and he knew that he was doing the right thing.

If doing the right thing causes you suffering, you're a lucky
person. I know that sounds crazy, but it's true. I admire those
who do what is right even when it isn't convenient or
comfortable. In Heaven, I'll be waiting to thank you personally for
it. Do the right thing, no matter what.

The One Who Knows,
>God

== == ==   == == == == == == == == ==

YOU'RE VALUABLE TO ME

Fear not, for I have redeemed you; I have summoned you by name; you are mine.

| Isaiah | 43:1 |

Dear Child of Mine,

>Some people love their cars. They're always washing and waxing them, and woe to the person who scratches their precious car!

You might think it's funny, but that's the way I am with you. When you ask Me into your life, that's when I "buy" you. You used to belong to yourself or to whoever you were living for. But now you're mine. A Porsche owner is not going to intentionally wreck his own car.

That's the way I am about you. You belong to Me, and I'm not going to let anyone hurt you. I'll take good care of you because you're so valuable to Me. So relax. Don't be afraid. You're Mine forever!

Love,
>God

== == ==   == == == == == == == == ==

THE ONE AND ONLY

**For who is God besides the Lᴏʀᴅ?
And who is the Rock except our God?**

Psalm   18:31

My Child,

>Do you realize that I am the *only* God? Satan is not a god; he's just a created being. I made him. Buddha is not a god; he was just a man, and now he's a man-made statue. Zeus is not God; he's just an ancient story. There is no God besides Me.

Some people say it doesn't matter what you believe so long as you believe sincerely. But I say, you can be sincerely wrong! So please get to know Me. The Bible is My book to tell you what I'm like. Jesus is My Son to show you how I act. The Holy Spirit is My messenger to bring Me into your heart.

No matter what you hear now, at the end of time when My Son returns, everyone will know and see that I really am who I say I am: the only living, true, all-powerful God. And the great news is, I love you!

Your Heavenly Father,
>God

== == ==   == == == == == == == == ==

A RIVER IN THE DESERT?

**For I will pour water on the thirsty land,
and streams on the dry ground.**

| | Isaiah | 44:3 | |

Dear Child of Mine,

>Do you ever feel "dry" inside? Do you feel tired of life? Tired of work? School? Friends? Tired of your town? Sounds like you could use a little refreshment!

If I can make an oasis in the middle of a physical desert, then surely I can bring life into your world. The more you open your heart to Me, the more I can send the rain of My Spirit to refresh you.

Cry out to Me right now. Don't hold anything back. Share your needs with Me. Ask Me to refresh you. I want to rain My love down on you. I want to give you hope again. Let Me revive you.

Your Living Water,
>God

== == == == == == == == == == == ==

IT'S TIME TO GROW UP

Break up your unplowed ground; for it is time to seek the LORD, until he comes and showers righteousness on you.

| | Hosea | 10:12 | |

My Child,

>Before a farmer plants a field, he plows it up. After plowing, the field just looks like a big pile of stirred-up dirt. It looks worse than before it was plowed. But that's the only way the seeds will ever take root.

I want to stir things up for you, too. If everything's perfect in your life right now, and you don't want it to improve, put down this book and stop seeking Me. But if you stick with Me, I'm going to change things. I want to plant good things in your life.

Trust Me, you're going to like the improvements I make. My changes will be worth it all. I promise!

Your Father,
>God

== == ==   == == == == == == == == ==

YOU HAVE FRIENDS IN HIGH PLACES

I have put my words in your mouth and
covered you with the shadow of my hand—I
who set the heavens in place, who laid
the foundations of the earth, and who
say to Zion, "You are my people."

Isaiah 51:16

Dear Child of Mine,

>It's true that I created the whole universe. It's true that I created
every animal, every plant, and every atom. But if that were the
end of the story, what good would I be to you?

Some people think I started the universe spinning, and now I'm
hiding in some corner, uninterested in your life. That's not true. I
hold you in My hand. You are My people, My tribe, My family.
Not only that, you are My child.

The same powerful God who made everything knows you by
name and wants to talk to you every day. You are so important
to Me. I love you!

Your Creator,
>God

== == ==   == == == == == == == == ==

I WASN'T BORN IN THE U.S.A.

**All nations will come and worship before you,
for your righteous acts have been revealed.**

| | Revelation | 15:4 | |

My Child,

>I'm not just the God of the United States. I don't just speak English. Actually, My Son, Jesus, was Jewish, and I speak every language on earth. Jesus lived in the Middle East and spoke a language called Aramaic.

All over the world right now there are people who worship My Son. People on every continent are praising Jesus in all sorts of different languages, using all sorts of different musical instruments, and dancing all sorts of ways.

Will all these people be in Heaven? You bet! If you don't like black people or white people or yellow people or red people or brown people, then you won't like it in Heaven. I love variety! That's why I made so many different races. So worship Me in your own way.

Your Creator,
>God

== == ==   == == == == == == == == ==

NOT YOUR TEACHER BUT YOUR MASTER

I will instruct you and teach you in the way you should go; I will counsel you and watch over you.

Psalm | 32:8

My Child,

>Long ago in Asia, when a young man who wanted to learn a skill, he would become an apprentice to a master rather than attending college. Night and day, the young man would work in the master's shop, watching, helping out, and practicing. The master would not just *tell* him how to work, but he would *show* him.

I want to be your Master. I want to see you more than once a week in Sunday School. I want to live with you, day in and day out. Isn't that how My Son, Jesus, taught His followers? I want you to come to Me every time you need help. Talk to Me and listen. Read in the Bible about the work I've done. Watch Me working in the world. I'm not your professor or your preacher. I am . . .

Your Master,
>God

== == ==   == == == == == == == == ==

HE'LL BE BACK

But our citizenship is in heaven. And we eagerly await a Savior from there, the Lord Jesus Christ.

Philippians 3:20

My Child,

>Jesus is My ambassador to the human race. He came down to earth two thousand years ago and said, "I know a country called Heaven. Anybody who follows Me can go there." Then Jesus returned to Heaven. His offer is still open.

But wait, there's more. Jesus is coming back to earth a second time to take all of Heaven's citizens with Him. However, the next time He comes, He won't appear as a baby. Instead, He'll be riding a white horse. The sky will split open, and He'll descend with massive fireworks. He's coming to bring My children home. If you've made Him your King, then that means He's coming back for you, too. Look for Him soon.

The One and Only,
>God

== == ==   == == == == == == == == ==

YOU'RE ONLY HUMAN

[The Lord] knows how we are formed,
he remembers that we are dust.

Psalm	103:14

Dear Child,

>I would make an A+ in biology class because I wrote the book on you. Not only do I know how you function physically, but I understand all of your emotions and thinking processes.

Since I created you, I know you inside out. I know what you can and cannot do. I don't expect you to do the impossible. I know you're going to fail at many things. You're just a person. So don't be so hard on yourself. A lot of times you expect more from yourself than I do.

When I live in you, I'll never fail. The impossible is My job, not yours. Your job is to be My friend. You're doing great, and I'm proud of you. Cut yourself some slack!

Your Creator,
>God

== == ==   == == == == == == == == ==

I WILL FREE YOU

Let [the prisoners] give thanks to the LORD
for his unfailing love and his wonderful
deeds for men, for he breaks down gates
of bronze and cuts through bars of iron.

Psalm   107:15-16

My Child,

>I hope you never see the inside of a prison, but imagine what it would be like. You'd get a desire to go see a movie. Nope, sorry. You're in prison. Hungry for some pizza? Too bad, all they're serving is soup. This is prison, remember?

When the U.S. prisoners of war were released from North Vietnam and returned to America, many of them got off the plane and kissed the ground. That is how thankful they were to be free. Prison bars aren't the only things that can steal your freedom. Anger, jealousy, worry, and fear will wrap you up in chains.

I want to free you from those negative emotions that keep you locked up. Give those feelings to Me, and then prepare to kiss the ground. I will free you.

Your Liberator,
>God

== == ==   == == == == == == == == ==

INVITE JESUS IN

Here I am! I stand at the door and knock.
If anyone hears my voice and opens the door,
I will come in and eat with him, and he with Me.

| Revelation | 3:20 |

My Child,

>Your heart is like a house where you spend every day. It's where you keep all your hopes and dreams, all your feelings and fears.

Some rooms in your heart hold shiny trophies. But other rooms hide the things you're most ashamed of. Because the lock is on the inside, you're the only one who can invite someone into your heart. My Son Jesus is standing outside the door of your heart, knocking. If you invite Him in, I will come in with Him.

Don't worry. We won't be shocked by anything We find. We already know what's in there. We want to help you do some house cleaning, one room at a time. We want to live with you in the house you call your heart, and We will make it a home. Will you open the door? It's up to you.

Your Lord,
>God

== == ==   == == == == == == == == ==

LIVE, IN PERSON, JESUS!

But we know that when he appears, we shall be like him, for we shall see him as he is.

| 1 John | 3:2 |

Dear Child,

>Don't you wish sometimes that you could just see Me in person? Wouldn't it have been great be alive when Jesus was on the earth in the flesh? Today people pray and strain their hearts to hear My answer. But back then, you could have asked Jesus a question and heard My answer in an audible voice.

The good news is, Jesus is coming back in person. You will be able to see and hear Him again. He is coming back to earth to take His family, those who love Him, to Heaven. And not only will they be able to see Him, but they will be like Him—pure and full of peace and joy. Are you ready to go?

Your Loving Father,
>God

== == ==   == == == == == == == == ==

REFERENCES

Unless otherwise indicated, all Scripture quotations are taken from the *Holy Bible, New International Version® NIV®.* Copyright © 1973, 1978, 1984 by International Bible Society. Used by permission of Zondervan Publishing House. All rights reserved.

Scripture quotations marked NKJV are taken from *The New King James Version* of the Bible. Copyright © 1979, 1980, 1982, by Thomas Nelson, Inc.

Verses marked THE MESSAGE are taken from *The Message,* copyright © 1993, 1994, 1995. Used by permission of NavPress Publishing Group.

Verses marked TLB are taken from *The Living Bible,* copyright © 1971. Used by permission of Tyndale House Publishers, Inc., Wheaton, Illinois 60189. All rights reserved.

Scripture quotations marked NCV are taken from *The Holy Bible, New Century Version,* copyright © 1987, 1988, 1991 by Word Publishing, Dallas, Texas 75039. Used by permission.

ABOUT THE AUTHORS

Claire Cloninger, winner of four Dove Awards for songwriting, also created the phenomenally successful musical *My Utmost for His Highest.* She has authored nine books, including best-sellers *A Place Called Simplicity* and *Dear Abba.*

Curt Cloninger, Claire's son, is employed as the Internet Administrator for Integrity Music and is the worship leader at the Mobile Vineyard Christian Fellowship. He spent two years in Youth With a Mission and has worked as a middle-school teacher, a high-school track coach, and a house parent in a children's home. He and his wife, Julie, are parents of nine-month-old Caroline.

If you have enjoyed this book, or if it has
impacted your life, we would like to hear from you.
Please contact us at:

Honor Books
Department E
P.O. Box 55388
Tulsa, Oklahoma 74155
Or by e-mail at *info@honorbooks.com*

Additional copies of this book
are available from your local bookstore.

Honor Books
Tulsa, Oklahoma